BENJAMIN FRANKLIN

LIVES AND LEGACIES

Larzer Ziff
MARK TWAIN

David S. Reynolds
WALT WHITMAN

Edwin S. Gaustad
ROGER WILLIAMS

Gale E. Christianson
ISAAC NEWTON

G. Edward White
OLIVER WENDELL HOLMES, JR.

Edwin S. Gaustad
BENJAMIN FRANKLIN

BENJAMIN FRANKLIN

Edwin S. Gaustad

OXFORD
UNIVERSITY PRESS

2006

OXFORD

UNIVERSITY PRESS

Oxford University Press, Inc., publishes works that
further Oxford University's objective of excellence
in research, scholarship, and education.

Oxford New York

Auckland Cape Town Dar es Salaam Hong Kong Karachi
Kuala Lumpur Madrid Melbourne Mexico City Nairobi
New Delhi Shanghai Taipei Toronto

With offices in

Argentina Austria Brazil Chile Czech Republic France Greece
Guatemala Hungary Italy Japan Poland Portugal Singapore
South Korea Switzerland Thailand Turkey Ukraine Vietnam

Copyright © 2006 by Edwin S. Gaustad

Published by Oxford University Press, Inc.
198 Madison Avenue, New York, NY 10016
www.oup.com

Oxford is a registered trademark of Oxford University Press

Library of Congress Cataloging-in-Publication Data
Gaustad, Edwin S. (Edwin Scott)
Benjamin Franklin / Edwin S. Gaustad.
p.cm. — (Lives and legacies)
Includes bibliographical references and index.
ISBN-13: 978-0-19-530535-7
ISBN-10: 0-19-530535-3
1. Franklin, Benjamin, 1706–1790.
2. Statesmen—United States—Biogaphy.
3. Scientists—United States—Biography.
4. Inventors—United States—Biography.
5. Printers—United States—Biography.
6. I. Title.
7. II. Series
E302.6F8G379 2005   973.3'092—dc22   2005033906

2 4 6 8 9 7 5 3 1
Printed in the United States of America
on acid-free paper

In gratitude for great marriages:
Scott and Mimi
Peggy and Stuart

ACKNOWLEDGMENTS

FOR THE WRITING OF THIS BOOK, Nancy Toff, vice president of Oxford University Press, served as catalyst, cheerleader, and perceptive critic. I owe her much. Others at the Press who have labored faithfully include the researcher for illustrations, the copy editor, and the project editor. Bringing it all together at the end, Helen Mules, senior editor in the trade division, utilized her talents and her experience most effectively, the final product bearing solid evidence of her judicious labors. I owe all of them much as well.

Contents

PROLOGUE   1

One

THE IMPROPER BOSTONIAN   5

Two

B. FRANKLIN, PRINTER   15

Three

DOCTOR FRANKLIN   33

Four

PENNSYLVANIA POLITICS   52

Five

THE ROAD TO SEPARATION   70

Six

WAR AND PEACE   88

Seven

NEW NATION AND AGED PATRIARCH   110

NOTES   127

FURTHER READING   133

INDEX   137

BENJAMIN FRANKLIN

Prologue

Among Benjamin Franklin's many talents was his gift for satire: making fun of the noble and the mighty, of the proud and pretentious, and on occasion even of the British Empire itself. But those who live by the satirical sword may die by it as well. In American literature, the only real competitor to Franklin in boundless, bubbling humor is Mark Twain. Both men had a built-in funny bone, so to speak, and for both no subject was too sacred, too solemn, to escape the bite of satire. Among the many subjects that Twain enjoyed making fun of was none other than Franklin himself.

Pretending to have been raised by a father who had read Franklin's *Autobiography* and to have been fatally infected by it, Twain bitterly complained, in a brief sketch from 1890 called "The Late Benjamin Franklin," that his boyhood had been ruined by having the model of Franklin held up to him day after day. Whenever Twain wanted to play, he was reminded of work that needed to be done, for Franklin was never idle. Whenever he spent a few pennies on a toy or a treat, he was sternly told that "a penny saved is a penny earned." And should he be so lazy as to stay in bed until 9 or 10 in the morning, then that perverse proverb was drilled into him:

Early to bed and early to rise

Makes a man healthy and wealthy and wise.

Twain scornfully adds, "As if it were any object to a boy to be healthy and wealthy and wise on such terms."

Franklin lived and wrote as he did, Twain declared, just so he could serve as a model to torment all future generations. Twain added that Franklin's simplest acts were contrived with a view to their being held up for the emulation of boys forever—boys who might otherwise have been happy. It was in this spirit, Twain jested, that he became the son of a soap-boiler; and probably for no other reason, he wrote, than to cast suspicion on the efforts of all future boys who tried to be anything who were not also the sons of soap-boilers. Twain observed, moreover, that Franklin would work all day and then sit up nights and pretend to be studying algebra by the light of a smoldering fire, so that all other boys would have to do the same or else have Benjamin Franklin thrown up to them.[1]

And so the master satirist was himself satirized. Twain's comments came long after Franklin's death, of course; otherwise, one can imagine a duel of satires that would forever enliven and enrich the literature of 19th-century America. But Franklin himself might well have sympathized with that imaginary boy who was forced to bow down before young Franklin as a Hero (with a capital *H*). In his best-selling *Almanack*, Franklin spoke of the three great destroyers of mankind as being "Plague, Famine, and Hero." The first two destroy people only, but the last "takes life and goods together." Heroes (think of a king on his throne or a Napoleon on his horse) infect and inflame the whole world, Franklin wrote, and are able to do so just because so many follow them passionately, if blindly.[2]

Like most men, Franklin appreciated praise more than blame. And like most men, he preferred to have his actions and thoughts looked at in their best light. But, unlike many men, Franklin kept himself and his deeds in perspective. His sense of humor helped him do that, as did his sense of proportion and of the transitory nature of life on this earth. Franklin had only a certain time on this world's stage: 1706 to 1790. But he made the very most of that time: in service to politics, to science, to literature, and—one might be so bold as to say—to the welfare of humankind.

Mark Twain's fears notwithstanding, one takes no great risk in getting to know Benjamin Franklin much better. The risk, rather, is in missing the opportunity to walk beside so amiable, so generous, so wise a companion.

One

THE IMPROPER BOSTONIAN

Up, sluggard, and waste not life; in the grave will be sleeping
enough.   —*Poor Richard's Almanack,* 1741

BENJAMIN FRANKLIN, BORN IN BOSTON IN 1706, WAS THE SON OF A
soap maker (Mark Twain did not make that up). His father, Josiah,
also made candles, and produced many children: 7 with his first
wife, Anne, and 10 with his second, Abiah, mother of Benjamin.
Not all the children survived into maturity, but most of them did,
so the impoverished Franklins spent much of their time trying to
feed many hungry mouths.

As Benjamin was the 10th and youngest son in the family, Josiah
initially thought of offering him as a tithe to the Congregational
Church as a student for the ministry. Tithing, or giving one-tenth of
one's income to the church, was widely practiced—or at least widely
preached—in many denominations. With this goal in mind, the father put his youngest son in grammar school when he was eight

years old. But it soon became clear that the cost of education, especially of a college education, would far outrun the family's means. So after two years in grammar school—the only formal education that this 10th son ever received—young Benjamin was brought into his father's shop as an apprentice and general handyman.

In his *Autobiography*, Benjamin describes his duties and his general distaste for them. "I was employed in cutting Wick for candles, filling the Dipping Mold, and the Mold for cast Candles, attending the Shop, going of Errands, etc. I dislik'd the Trade and had a strong Inclination for the Sea; but my father declar'd against it." Though he was not permitted to go to sea, Benjamin took advantage of the waters around Boston to become an excellent swimmer and a skillful handler of boats. He also discovered in himself around the age of 10 or so the ability to organize other boys in various pursuits, some legitimate and others—such as "borrowing" stones intended for a new house to build a small wharf for fishing—less so.[1]

But if he did not want to be a candle maker and could not go to sea, as one of his older brothers had, what occupation awaited him? By the time he was 12, he had the answer: he would be a printer. When his brother James returned from England with a press and type to set up business in Boston, Benjamin—at his father's urging—agreed to serve as James's apprentice until he reached age 21. In colonial America, this type of vocational training was the most common way of acquiring the skills that enabled one to earn a living. One began as an apprentice, moved on to become a journeyman (at better wages), and ended as a master. This is the path that Benjamin seemed destined to follow, but all did not unfold smoothly.

However, this arrangement did give the young apprentice access to books: books that came into the shop for one reason or another, books that he could borrow and return "soon and clean," and books that he could buy in very cheap editions. He first bought, for example, the works of John Bunyan, the author of the Puritan epic *Pilgrim's Progress*. After reading quickly through those little volumes, he sold them in order to buy more books. Because he worked all day, he did his reading mainly at night, or in an abbreviated lunchtime. He read whatever he could get his hands on, and later regretted that the family library consisted mainly of books treating religious controversies, which he found unworthy of his attention then—and ever after.[2]

But Benjamin in these early years did more than just read: he gave himself an education, by learning arithmetic from a simple text, navigation in the same manner, and how to write. Thanks to the printing shop, his punctuation was already in good shape, but his prose needed improvement. When Benjamin came across the essays of English authors such as Joseph Addison and Richard Steele, he decided to use them as models for his own writing. He would copy what they wrote, then take an argument of his own and try to put it in their elegant style. Or, he would translate what they had to say into poetry (bad poetry, he admitted); then, when he had forgotten the original prose, proceed to put his poetry back into worthy prose.[3]

While improving his style and his grammar, Benjamin learned something of the art of argumentation from reading the classical authors of ancient Greece and Rome. In his debates with boyhood friends, he was very assertive and quite positive in defense of his position. But he soon learned how to be modest in argument: to say, "It seems to me," or "I conceive," or "I apprehend a thing to be so." Also, he found one could often argue even more effectively not by making firm declarations, but by asking subtle and gentle questions. His opponents would soon make concessions from which they could find no logical way out. Frequently, in this way, he could win an argument and yet not lose a friend.[4]

By the time he was 16, Benjamin was ready to try his hand at some serious composition. At this point, James was publishing a newspaper, the *New-England Courant,* and the paper was often hungry for material. Writing under a false name, "Silence Dogood," as was often the custom in the 18th century, the teenager wrote 14 short essays for the *Courant.* These pieces reveal, among other things, how successful his self-education program had been. Franklin wrote with a smoothness and charm that concealed the author's youth as much as the pseudonym concealed his identity.

In a clever satire on Harvard College, for example, Benjamin indicated how every New England "peasant," if he could possibly afford it, aspired to send his son to this great "Temple of Learning." The parent considered only whether he could afford the education, ignoring completely the capacity of the young man to benefit from it. So often, Franklin asserted, the lack of genius in the Harvard student guaranteed the folly of the expensive education.

"They learn little more," Franklin wrote, "than how to carry themselves handsomely, and enter a Room genteely, (which might as well be acquir'd at a Dancing School)." Franklin added that after the "Abundance of Trouble and Charge," some ill-suited scholars graduated "as great Blockheads as ever, only more proud and self-conceited." All those New England peasants who could not afford to send their sons to Harvard, Benjamin's father included, must have enjoyed the great joke, even as they looked forward to the next words from Silence Dogood—which had been promised to appear every two weeks.[5]

In another issue, Silence Dogood—who was presented as a widow and mother recently arrived in the colonies—considered the question of female education. Women are quite capable of learning, as capable as men, the author argued, and only artificial barriers prevent women from reaching the same intellectual level as men. Women "are taught to read indeed, and perhaps to write their Names, or so; and that is the Height of a Women's Education." If women are reproached for idleness or folly or ignorance, he wrote, men have only themselves to blame. Moreover, "if Knowledge and Understanding" were useless additions for women to possess, "God Almighty would have never given them Capacities, for he made nothing Needless."[6] In this argument, as in many others, Franklin was well ahead of his time. Harvard classes became coeducational only in 1943.

Benjamin's choice of the name Silence Dogood was probably influenced by the 1710 publication of *Essays to Do Good* by Boston's leading Puritan clergyman, Cotton Mather. In later life, Franklin indicated that this work had much influence on him, though Mather's biblically based Puritan theology he left largely behind.[7] Reading as widely as he did among the works of freethinkers in England—that is, those who rejected inspired scripture and appealed only to reason—Benjamin, while still in his teens, turned away from the Congregational orthodoxy that his father urged upon him. The young man created his own religion, rather than agreeing to any widely accepted creed or the defending of any churchly doctrine. From his reading and reflection, he soon came to value morality over dogma, deeds over pious words, reason over revelation.[8]

His published criticism of the clergy and of the churches, however, was necessarily subtle and indirect, for his brother James and his newspaper ran into difficulties with the authorities for being openly critical of both ecclesiastical and civil authorities. Indeed, James was arrested for hinting at some collusion between local

THE New-England Courant.

From MONDAY March 26. to MONDAY April 2. 1722.

Honour's a Sacred Tye, the Law of Kings,
The Noble Mind's Distinguishing Perfection,
That aids and strengthens Virtue where it meets her,
And Imitates her Actions where she is not,
It ought not to be sported with ——————   Cato.

To the Author of the New-England Courant.

SIR,   Sagadahock, March 20.

HONOUR is a Word that Sounds big and makes a most ravishing Entrance into Men's Ears, while a Just and proper Notion of it, is mistaken by most, and the Rules and Measures of it, are comply'd with but by few.

Hence it comes to pass, that some who make a conspicuous Figure in the World, (thro' their Ignorance of this Noble Principle,) falsly imagine themselves to be treading in the Paths of Honour, while they are but greedily pursuing their Ambitious Designs, and Impatiently Gratifying their Lusts of Pride and Covetousness.

Honour indeed, according to the vulgar Notion of it, is nothing more than an empty Name. The Actions of many Men, speak their Sentiments of it ; and render it Obvious, that they suppose it to consist only in Flattering Titles, and high Posts and Preferments, be they Acquir'd in the most Shameful and Dishonourable Ways. But how often do such Precipitate themselves into Open Shame ? and when they fondly imagine they have grasp'd the Airy Phantom, and arriv'd to the utmost Pitch of Honour, Behold, it Vanishes into nothing, perishes even in the using, and leaves a lasting Brand of Infamy on their Memory.

Now seeing nothing is more pernicious, than a Principle of Action not rightly apprehended, it may not be improper, First, To hint at some Things, which have the Shadow and Appearance of Honour, but in reality are Infamous and Dishonourable ; and Then, to give some brief Description of this Superiour Principle.

With respect then to Posts of Honour and Honourary Titles, (and some Men have no other Idea of Honour than what results from such Empty Names as these,) it may be said in the Words of an Ingenious Writer, " But whatever Wealth " and Dignities Men may arrive at, they ought to consider, " that every one stands as a Blot in the Annals of his Coun- " try, who arrives at the Temple of Honour, by any other " Way than through that of Vertue". He that advanceth himself to Posts of Honour, by cursed Bribery, or sordid Flattery, or any other base and unworthy Arts, lays his Honour in the Dust, and Exposes himself to lasting Infamy and Reproach. It is also highly Dishonourable for a Man, when any particular Accomplishment is requisite to Qualify him

break, that they may attain their Ends ? Too many such there are, (says Mr. Dummer, in his Defence of the N. E. Charters, pag. 42.) who are contented to be Saddled themselves, provided they may Ride others under the chief Rider.

Men of Tyrannical Principles, with what abhorrence are they to be Look'd on, by all who have any Sense of Honour ? Such, it may be presum'd, had they Power equal to their Will, would soon, not only Sacrifice Honour, and Conscience, but even all Mankind, to their Voracious Appetites. They are to be Esteem'd, (as Dr. Cotton Mather calls them) the Basest of Men. Such Sons of Nimrod, Nero, & old Lewis, are viler than the Earth they tread on ; it groans under them as an Intolerable Plague, and insupportable Burthen. Tyranny and Honour, cannot Reign together in the same Breast.

And (to mention nothing more) it is very Dishonourable, for Men to make rash and hasty Promises, relating to any Thing Wherein the Interest of the Publick is nearly concern'd, and then to say, they will retain their Integrity forever, or till Doomsday, pretending it is for fear of violating their Word and Honour. The Talents, Interest, or Experience of such Men (says one) make them very often useful in all Parties, and at all Times. They Ridicule every Thing as Romantick, that comes in Competition with their present Interests ; and treat those Persons as Visionaries, who dare stand up in a corrupt Age, for what has not its immediate Reward annexed to it.

But let us now change the Scene, and see what true Honour is. And no doubt, the reverse of what has been said is truly Honourable. True HONOUR, (as a Learned Writer defines it) is the Report of Good and Vertuous Actions, issuing from the Conscience into the Discovery of the PEOPLE with whom we live, and which (by a Reflection on our selves) gives us the Testimony of what others believe concerning us, and to the Soul becomes a great Satisfaction. True Honour, (says another) tho' it be a different Principle from Religion, is that which Produces the same Effects. The Lines of Action, tho' drawn from different Parts, terminate in the same Point. Religion Embraces Vertue, as it is enjoin'd by the Laws of GOD ; Honour, as it is Graceful and Ornamental to Humane Nature. The Religious Man fears, the Man of Honour scorns to do an ill Action. A Noble Soul, would rather die, than commit an Action that should make his Children Blush, when he is in his Grave, and be look'd upon as a Reproach to those who shall live a Hundred Years after him.

In a Word, He is the Honourable Man, who is Influenc'd and Acted by a Publick Spirit, and fir'd with a Generous Love to Mankind in the worst of Times ; Who lays aside his private Views, and foregoes his own Interest, when it comes in competition with the Publick ; Who dare adhere to the Cause of Truth, and Manfully Defend the Liberties of his Country, when boldly Invaded, and Labour to retrieve them when they are Lost. Yea, the Man of Honour, (when contracted sordid Spirits desert the Cause of Vertue and the Publick) will stand himself alone, and (like Atlas) bear up

The February 11, 1723, issue of the *New-England Courant* is the first to bear the name of Benjamin Franklin as editor. This arrangement with his brother James lasted only a few weeks, as James again took charge of the paper when young Benjamin fled to Philadelphia in September 1723.
Courtesy of the Massachusetts Historical Society, Boston

authorities and pirates in or around Boston Harbor; he was briefly imprisoned in Boston. During this time, young Benjamin took over the editorial responsibilities of the *New-England Courant.*

In its pages he argued for freedom of thought and freedom of speech, as these, he declared, were the right of every man and of every people. He wrote, "Whoever would overthrow the liberty of a nation must begin by subduing the freeness of speech."[9] James, one might think, would be grateful for this defense, as well as to his younger brother for assuming all the burdens of running the newspaper while he was in prison. But Benjamin, now 17, had moved beyond the lowly status of apprentice, thus appearing as a threat to the master.

Such was James's agitation that he, though normally an even-tempered man, boxed and cuffed his younger brother. This behavior, Benjamin reported, "I took extremely amiss." Though acknowledging that he might have been "too saucy and provoking," Benjamin found the situation increasingly intolerable. The brothers took their disagreement to their father, who generally found in Benjamin's favor, which only irritated James further. But in this case their father sided with James. When Benjamin resolved to leave his brother's employ anyway, James took the unbrotherly step of visiting all the other printers in Boston to ensure that they would not take the young apprentice—still under a contract of indenture, or obligatory service to his brother—into any of their shops.[10]

So what to do and where to go? Young Benjamin's life had reached a turning point that threatened to become a stopping point. Benjamin knew that he would have to depart Boston in secret. And so it was that a young friend persuaded a ship's captain that young Benjamin had gotten a "naughty girl" pregnant and had, therefore, to slip away. "So I sold some of my Books to raise a little Money," Franklin later wrote, and "was taken on board privately, and as we had a fair Wind, in three days I found myself in New York, near 300 Miles from home." He concluded somberly that here he was, "a Boy of but 17, without the least Recommendation to or Knowledge of any Person in the Place, and with very little Money in my Pocket." His first timid steps toward an independent life did not seem all that promising.[11]

Hooped Petticoats and the Folly of Fashion

Franklin first tried his hand at writing by composing entertaining pieces for his brother's newspaper, the New-England Courant. *He wrote a series of letters to the editor under the name of Silence Dogood, assuming the role of a recent female immigrant to Boston. When Franklin was 16, he wrote an essay, published in June 1722, about the current fashion of Boston ladies. They were dressing themselves in very wide, very awkward, and—from Franklin's point of view—very absurd petticoats.*

I cannot dismiss this Subject without some Observations on a particular Fashion now reigning, among my own Sex, the most immodest and inconvenient of any the Art of Woman has invented, namely, that of Hoop-Petticoats. By these they are incommoded in their General and Particular Calling, and therefore cannot answer the Ends of either necessary or ornamental Apparel. These monstrous topsy-turvy Mortar Pieces, are neither fit for the Church, the Hall, or the Kitchen; and if a Number of them were well mounted on Noddles Island, they would look more like Engines of War for bombarding the Town, than Ornaments of the Fair Sex. An honest Neighbour of mine, happening to be in Town some time since on a publick Day inform'd me, that he saw four

Gentlewomen with Hoops half mounted in a Balcony, as they withdrew to the Wall, to the great Terror of the Militia, who (he thinks) might attribute their irregular Volleys to the formidable Appearance of the Ladies Petticoats.

I assure you, Sir, I have but little Hopes of perswading my Sex, by this Letter, utterly to relinquish the extravagant Foolery, and Indication of Immodesty, in this monstrous Garb of theirs; but I would at least desire them to lessen the Circumference of their Hoops, and leave it with them to consider, Whether they, who pay no Rates or Taxes, ought to take up more Room in the King's High-Way, than the Men, who yearly contribute to the Support of the Government.

I am, Sir,
Your Humble Servant,
SILENCE DOGOOD

Two

B. FRANKLIN, PRINTER

Keep thy shop, and thy shop will keep thee.
—*Poor Richard's Almanack,* 1735

FRANKLIN DID NOT LINGER LONG IN NEW YORK CITY. ATTEMPTING to find employment there, he applied to the only printer, William Bradford, who advised him that he did not have sufficient work to require a helper. But he then helpfully added that his son, a printer in Philadelphia, had recently lost his chief assistant, and that Franklin could very likely take his place. So Franklin set out, by water, for Philadelphia—a mere 100 miles away. Colonial roads were in such primitive condition that travel by sloop along the coast was generally preferred. But this route proved, in Franklin's case, to be hardly any better.

Storms ripped the rotten sails of his vessel to bits, driving the small boat toward Long Island. One drunken passenger fell overboard, only to be rescued by Franklin. Franklin and the skipper sought refuge from the rain as they slept fitfully through the foul night. Franklin fell ill, but by morning was sufficiently recovered to take a ferry to the mainland, about 50 miles north of Burlington, New Jersey. From there, he proceeded on foot to Burlington, but was so tired by noon that he stopped at a small roadside inn to spend the night, "beginning now to wish that I had never left home," as he noted in his *Autobiography*. The next day, somewhat refreshed, he made it all the way to Burlington, only to discover that no regular boat left for Philadelphia until the next Tuesday, and this was Saturday.

Resigned to a long stay at yet another inexpensive inn, he strolled along the Delaware River that night and had the good luck to spy a small boat floating by that was headed for Philadelphia. Invited to join the company, Franklin helped to row, there being no wind to fill the sails. "About Midnight not having yet seen the City, some of the Company were Confident we must have pass'd it, and would row no farther." So they pulled into the shelter of a small creek to spend the remainder of the night. The next morning, when they emerged from the creek, they saw Philadelphia just ahead, and docked at the Market Street Wharf at about 8 or 9 o'clock on Sunday morning.[1]

Franklin's arrival in Philadelphia is a permanent fixture of early American history and myth: his bewilderment and loneliness, his purchase of three great "Puffy Rolls," his "most awkward and ridiculous appearance," and the amusement of Deborah Read—his future wife—as she watched this strange youth walking down the street with a bread roll under each arm as he hungrily consumed the third. In evaluating Franklin's account in the *Autobiography*, it is useful to remember these circumstances: a homesick 17-year-old boy, a weary survivor of a miserable journey by sea and by land, bereft of friends and funds, and anxious beyond words over what turn of fortune might lay ahead. Things could not get worse; they had to get better. He had eaten some bread; he had a prospect of employment; and he found a quiet Quaker meeting, where he promptly fell asleep. Then he found a suitable inn where he ate and slept some more, so by Monday morning, October 7, 1723, he was ready to confront the commercial bustle of Philadelphia.[2]

The town in which Franklin now found himself was the port of entry into the large colony of Pennsylvania, founded only about 40 years before the arrival of the young man from Boston. William Penn, the colony's founder, was a Quaker who initially saw this vast tract of land in North America as a refuge for English Quakers who were persecuted in England and virtually everywhere else. But Pennsylvania was open to all, with religious freedom guaranteed to all. And the immigrants poured in: from England and Germany, from Ireland and Wales, and even from neighboring colonies. Pennsylvania's farmland proved to be very fertile. Land was generously offered to new arrivals at prices that could be paid off with comparative ease over a period of years. And in town, artisans and craftsmen could set up shop immediately and, with talent and hard labor, soon prosper—as Philadelphia itself did.

If Boston was America's leading metropolis in the 17th century, Philadelphia would become the country's major city in the 18th. In the 1720s, it was on the rise, and energetic, gifted young men could rise with it—as Benjamin Franklin so clearly did. Compared with Massachusetts, Pennsylvania was a much more open society: open to commercial and agricultural opportunities, open to new ideas, open to innovation and experimentation. In the realm of religion, the contrast could not be more striking.

In the early 1660s, Boston—still very much dominated by the Puritans or Congregationalists—hanged four Quakers for their stubborn heresies; in the 1680s, Quakers were in charge of the cultural and political life of Pennsylvania. In this decade the Quakers, or Society of Friends, were only a generation old, but they had become conspicuous because of their emphasis on pacifism and equality of the sexes, their disdain of a professional ministry, and their services, called "meetings." These meetings were kept in silence unless someone was inspired by the Holy Spirit to speak. (In Franklin's first visit to a Quaker meeting on the Sunday of his arrival, no one was so inspired—so Franklin could sleep.)[3]

The following Monday he sought employment. He went first to the print shop of Andrew Bradford, to which he had been directed by the elder Bradford in New York. Franklin discovered to his dismay that a new helper had recently been hired. But the courteous and hospitable Bradford gave the young man breakfast and told him of another printer in town, Samuel Keimer, who had just set himself up in business. Keimer, however, like Bradford, did not need a full-time employee, but both printers promised to give the young man part-time work to help him get by. "Gaining Money by my Industry and Frugality," Franklin noted in the *Autobiography*, he soon "lived very agreeably, forgetting Boston as much as I could." Despite his youth, Franklin soon recognized that he knew more about the printing business, to say nothing of the English language, than either of his employers. Opportunities beckoned.[4]

Then a strange interlude delayed him from immediately seizing the opportunities that Philadelphia offered. The governor of the colony, Sir William Keith, heard of Franklin's recent arrival and concluded, Franklin reported, that he was "a young Man of promising Parts." When the governor came to Philadelphia from

New Castle—seat of the government for Pennsylvania's "lower counties," now Delaware—he invited Franklin to join him for a glass of Madeira wine in a nearby tavern. Franklin was both flattered and hopeful concerning what this glass of Madeira might lead to. It led, unfortunately, to a con job.

Keith promised to set up young Franklin in business and turn government printing affairs his way. He also suggested that Franklin return to his father in Boston to obtain some financial assistance in this enterprise. Franklin expressed doubts, but Sir William grandly assured him that he would provide a letter to his father that would win his support. So Franklin set out, again by water, and again encountered all sorts of difficulties. After two weeks, he finally arrived in Boston, to call upon his family after an absence of about seven months. All were glad to see him, he reported, except his brother James. The father considered Keith's letter carefully, but at length declined the offer contained therein. "I being in his Opinion too young to be trusted with the Management of a Business so important, and for which the Preparation must be so expensive," Franklin recalled in the *Autobiography*.

Franklin parted lovingly from his mother and father, and this time with their blessing made his way back to Philadelphia. Governor Keith, however, was not through with promises and proposals for Franklin. If Franklin's father would not set up his son in business, then Keith claimed he would do it himself. All he needed from Franklin was a list of equipment, paper, and type required for a successful enterprise, and Keith would take care of it. Franklin dutifully drew up such a list, amounting to about £100 sterling in materials, and presented it to Keith, who suggested that all might be more effectively procured if Franklin himself went to London to make the purchases. Keith would provide letters of credit, and all would be carried out with maximum efficiency and economy. So reasonable and so generous an offer could hardly be refused.[5]

As the government-sponsored annual ship from Philadelphia to London did not leave for many months, Franklin kept busy in Keimer's print shop and in intensifying his friendship with Deborah Read. Franklin initially lodged with Deborah's family, and their friendship began when she, in amusement, watched him eat those great puffy rolls on his first Sunday in the city. He even considered marrying her, but the young lady's mother thought that as both parties were only 18, and as Franklin was soon off for London, it would be better to wait.

Finally, the day for sailing arrived. Franklin had called upon the governor several times for those letters of credit and was put off each time, but he was solemnly assured that they would be on the ship. The ship sailed, but the letters were not on board, nor did the governor apparently ever intend that they would be. Franklin had been duped: it would not happen again. His opinion of Sir William Keith plummeted, though his final judgment was gently phrased: "He wish'd to please everybody; and having little to give, he gave Expectations."[6]

Franklin arrived in London on Christmas Eve, 1724, once again with no employment, no friends, and very limited funds. But he had more confidence in himself at this point, even if somewhat less confidence in his fellowman. He found a job in a printing shop, of course, and resumed his program of self-education: more books to read; leading English authors to meet; and more novel, or even radical, ideas to entertain. After setting in type a British book on natural religion (a religion based only on nature and reason), Franklin composed *A Dissertation on Liberty and Necessity,* in which his freethinking went further than ever before, and further than it would go again. The 18-year-old brashly argued that in this world there was much necessity (that is, absence of genuine free will), hardly any liberty, and no point whatsoever to traditional religion. He printed only a few copies of this small tract, and burned most of those, regretting this youthful venture as one of the errata of his life.[7]

After a year and a half in London, Franklin returned to Philadelphia in October 1727. He entered briefly into a small retail business with a Quaker friend, but then soon returned to Keimer's print shop. Within a year, he was ready to leave Keimer in order to go into the printing business with another of Keimer's employees, Hugh Meredith. In 1729 he bought out Keimer's newspaper, the *Pennsylvania Gazette,* which he soon made into the colony's most widely read newspaper. He accomplished this through public offices that he held and private "Industry" that he regularly practiced.

With a loan, he managed to buy out Meredith's share in the partnership so that by 1730, at age 24, Franklin was his own man in Philadelphia's printing world. He even became Pennsylvania's official printer early that same year. The abundant business enabled him to open a shop on the side that sold stationery, ink, pens, pencils, and books on virtually any subject. Sir William Keith had sidetracked Franklin, but only temporarily.

Industry paid off, handsomely. But Franklin would not let the welcome profits divert him from his steady attention to self-improvement. And if he could make such striking improvement on his own, why not invite others to join him in a program of mutual education and, as necessary, mutual assistance?

Soon after his return from London, he proceeded to form a discussion club of like-minded, energetic, and ambitious young men who would meet every Friday evening. The group—taking the name Junto, possibly from the Spanish word for fraternity—saw the whole intellectual world open to them for discussion and improved understanding. Franklin laid down a few rules to help ensure freedom of inquiry, the point of discussion being not a victory but a search. Once every three months each member would orally present an essay of his own composition for the benefit of those assembled. The Junto included a great mixture: a surveyor, a shoemaker (but with a love of reading), an official scribe, a mathematician (who did not last long), a poet, a merchant, and several others. The only qualifications were a thirst for knowledge and an open mind. The Junto, which continued for decades, Franklin happily reported, was the "best School of Philosophy, Morals, and Politics that then existed in the Province."[8]

At Franklin's suggestion, members of the Junto brought a good many of their books to the room where they met, so that their fellows could consult them. This experiment worked for a time, but was soon abandoned. Franklin launched a far more permanent venture, the Library Company of Philadelphia, in 1731. Its 50 members (later expanded to 100) contributed 10 shillings a year, and pledged to continue giving that amount for 50 years. Members, no longer dependent on importing books from England, could draw on the resources of the ever-growing library, and soon "reading became fashionable." This subscription library, "my first Project of a public Nature," proved a source of continuing pride to Franklin, and to the citizens of Philadelphia down to the present.

This, the first subscription library in North America, had many imitators over the years, even as the original grew stronger and stronger. And the whole point? "These Libraries have improv'd the general Conversation of the Americans," Franklin noted in his

Autobiography, and "made the common Tradesmen and Farmers as intelligent as most Gentleman from other Countries." He then added that the libraries "perhaps have contributed in some degree to the Stand so generally made throughout the Colonies in Defense of their Privileges." Franklin thought that books contained the potential solution to most problems in human lives or in nations. They had certainly proved to be so in his own experience.[9]

Among the issues that the Junto considered were many related to morality. As was so often the case, once the matter came up, Franklin thought about it more deeply and more systematically than most. In 1733 he decided that one must work hard in order to attain virtue; it would not happen easily or without diligent and sustained effort. The trick was to practice virtue so steadily that it became a habit. But how might one manage that? Franklin's plan was to keep a little book where he would record his faithfulness to each of the 13 virtues that he had identified: temperance, silence, order, resolution, frugality, industry, sincerity, justice, moderation, cleanliness, tranquility, chastity, and humility.

For a week, he would concentrate on one virtue. On a single page he set down the days in the week, and then each day he would record with a black mark every infraction against the particular virtue. He could get through his whole list in 13 weeks, and manage to do the entire sequence four times a year. "I was surprised to find myself so much fuller of Faults than I had imagined," he wrote in the *Autobiography,* "but I had the Satisfaction of seeing them diminish." Franklin would carry his little book with him wherever he went, at home and abroad, as several witnesses testified.

Making progress in his effort to acquire virtue as a steady habit, he reduced his self-examination from four times a year to once a year, then to once in several years, until the noting and marking could be omitted entirely. "But I always carried my little Book with me," he noted. It is easy to ridicule this strenuous effort in moral accounting, but to dismiss it entirely would be to miss an essential element in Franklin's unceasing effort at self-improvement.[10]

Meanwhile, two episodes in Franklin's personal life should be noted. Around 1730, an illegitimate son, William, was born to a woman never identified. Franklin acknowledged the boy's paternity, and raised this child, his firstborn, with tenderness and care.[11] Later that year, Franklin married Deborah Read, who had earlier (while Franklin was in London) married John Rogers. After a few months, Rogers abandoned his wife and disappeared from the pages of history. Because Rogers could not be located for purposes of a divorce, Franklin and Deborah Read contracted a common-law marriage: that is, by living together, the marriage came to be recognized by custom and common consent.

Though Deborah had a limited education, and though she joined Franklin in few of his public endeavors, the affection between them appears to have been genuine and long-lasting. He found her as frugal as himself, he wrote in the *Autobiography*, adding, "She assisted me chearfully in my Business, folding & stitching Pamphlets, tending Shop, purchasing old Linen Rags for the Paper-makers, &c. &c." A son, Franky, was born in 1732, but died four years later.[12] Then in 1743, a daughter, Sarah (known as Sally), was born. She grew to maturity and enjoyed an affectionate relationship with her father.[13]

In 1731 Franklin joined the Masons, an affiliation that he maintained for the rest of his life, both in Europe and America. The Masons, or Freemasons, are a secret fraternity dedicated to mutual assistance and brotherly support. Never one to do anything timidly or only halfway, in 1734 Franklin published *The Consti-*

tutions of the Free-Masons, the first Masonic book printed in America; he was also elected grand master of his lodge, St. John's, in Philadelphia. And in 1749 he was chosen grand master of the Masons for all Pennsylvania. The Masons were a source of companionship for the very social Franklin, who missed the society of the church, which he had forsaken.[14]

In the early 1730s, he had continued to attend the Presbyterian Church in Philadelphia, Presbyterianism being the rough equivalent of the Congregationalism that he knew in Boston. But he grew increasingly impatient with the Presbyterian obsession with what he considered minor points of doctrine. So many ministers seemed interested only in making good Presbyterians instead of good citizens.

When one clergyman, Samuel Hemphill, concentrated on preaching morality—to Franklin's delight—he was reproved by his clerical peers for not paying enough attention to doctrine. Franklin once again resorted to satire, in an imaginary "Dialogue Between Two Presbyterians," published in the *Pennsylvania Gazette* in 1735. Faith without works is not only dead, Franklin's spokesman declared, but after a time such faith begins to rot and smell. "Is Virtue Heresy?" the pro-Franklin debater incredulously asked, or is "Universal Benevolence False Doctrine, that any of us should keep away from Meeting because it is preached there?"

When Hemphill was found guilty of heresy by a commission of the Synod of Philadelphia and was dismissed from the church, Franklin was both irritated and angered. He used the power of the press—his press—to ridicule the "zealous Presbyterians" and to defend the moralizing Hemphill. The whole episode left a bad taste in many mouths, and certainly in Franklin's. It turned him away from the dogmatism of the churches, and from public religious disputes. Surprisingly, however, a few years later he supported the popular preacher and orator George Whitefield. Franklin admired Whitefield's ability to draw large crowds and to proclaim, extemporaneously, an open and nondogmatic gospel. He also printed Whitefield's sermons and journals, to the great satisfaction of the young Anglican orator and to the great profit of the enterprising Philadelphia printer.[15]

Printing remained Franklin's principal occupation and the source of his steadily growing income. He printed official documents, paper currency, news accounts from abroad, letters to the editor of the *Gazette* (many of which he encouraged personally), and items from his own pen. Not everything that he printed found universal or even wide approval. So in 1731 he wrote his *Apology for Printers,* in which he explained the unique position of those in his profession—compared, let us say, to that of the carpenter, shoemaker, tailor, or tradesman. These persons, he asserted, can work for customers of many sorts without offending any of them. "The Merchant may buy and sell with Jews, Turks, Hereticks, and Infidels of all sorts, and get Money by every one of them, without giving Offense to the most orthodox, of any sort." But not the printer, Franklin complained. He is obliged to respect public opinion, and yet "public opinion" is so diverse. "The Opinions of Men are almost as various as their Faces," Franklin concluded.

In his *Apology* Franklin argued that some men, quite unreasonably, expect to be pleased with everything that is printed. They even think "that nobody ought to be pleas'd but themselves." Whereas, he noted, the printer has been taught that when controversies arise, both sides "ought equally to have the Advantage of being heard by the Publick." Obviously, then, the printer cannot be thought of as one who agrees with everything he prints. If some readers argue that printers should print only that with which they agree, then, Franklin asserted, "an End would thereby be put to Free Writing, and the World would have nothing to read but what happen'd to be the Opinions of Printers." If the printer's principal aim is not to give offense, "there would be very little printed." Franklin concluded that angry patrons may in the heat of argument demand he give up his profession, but, said the besieged Philadelphia printer, "I shall not burn my Press and melt my Letters."[16]

Indeed, Franklin fought back with ever more successful ventures, none more so than *Poor Richard's Almanack*. Launched in 1732, this publication proved to be enormously popular. In the colonial period, an almanac was a staple in nearly every home. It predicted the

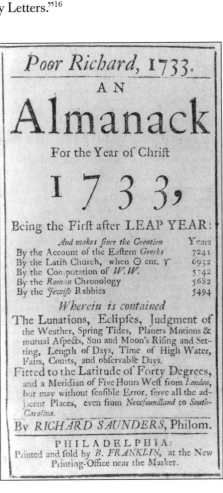

Published under the pseudonym of Richard Saunders, Franklin's very popular *Almanack* was filled with useful information such as tides, temperatures, and times for the rising and setting of the sun and moon, as well as witty epigrams. *The Rosenbach Museum & Library, Philadelphia*

weather, recorded the major events of the previous year, and gave the phases of the moon and the times of the tides. But if all this sounds rather monotonous and humdrum, Franklin enlivened his almanac with witty sayings and insightful proverbs. Not all of these, as he readily admitted, were original, for why—he explained— should he use his bad words when better ones were already at hand?

His almanac, then, was intended to be "both entertaining and useful," and its success almost overwhelmed him. He sold 10,000 copies a year, in a colony whose total population in the 1730s was less than 15,000. The demand was such, he admitted in the *Autobiography* that "I reap'd considerable Profit from it." Franklin continued to publish this popular piece every year until he left for England in 1757.[17]

Many generations later, the wit and wisdom of the *Almanack* continues to entertain, even if the words on tides and weather are hopelessly obsolete. "Love your neighbor," Franklin advised, "but don't pull down your hedge." One often-repeated proverb is this: "Fish and visitors smell in three days." When a proverb appeared in many forms, Franklin preferred the briefest: "He that falls in love with himself will have no rivals." To the young people among his readers, his suggestion was, "Keep your eyes wide open before marriage, and half shut afterwards." The epitaph to a long, or long-suffering, marriage read this way: "Here my poor Bridget's corpse doth lie,—She is at rest, and so am I." Sharing a typical colonial suspicion of doctors, Franklin observed that "He's a fool who makes his doctor his heir." Nor could he resist a few digs at institutional religion. For example, "Many have quarreled about religion that never practiced it." Or "None preaches better than the ant, and she says nothing." Finally, "Serving God is doing good to man, but praying is thought an easier service and therefore is more generally chosen."[18]

Of course, the *Almanack* was only one of many projects that kept Franklin and his helpers in the printing shop busy. In 1737 he was appointed postmaster of Philadelphia, a position that gave him first access to news from abroad, and his *Pennsylvania Gazette* took every advantage of this opportunity. Much later, in 1753, he was appointed joint deputy postmaster general for all the colonies, a position that extended his horizons and his influence well beyond the borders of Pennsylvania. He regarded this appointment as no mere political plum, but rather as an opportunity to give the colonies their first efficient postal system, which extended from Maine to Georgia. He visited most of the colonial offices, inspected the roads and the ferries—all with an eye to keeping the mail moving regularly and rapidly.[19]

Decades earlier, in 1734, he had been appointed the public printer for Delaware and New Jersey, and a bit later for Maryland and then New York as well. In 1736 Franklin accepted an appointment as clerk of the Pennsylvania Assembly, a position he held for 15 years. In this role, he had early access to legislative matters, even as his postmaster appointment continued to give him early access to events beyond his own colony. Not even Franklin could keep up with these many printing opportunities all by himself. Franklin formed partnerships with other printers not just in his Philadelphia business, but in the other colonies as well. He set up printers here and there in order to share in the profits that would eventually come. He even formed a partnership in the 1750s that would enable him to bring out his newspaper in a German edition to reach a growing readership among the Germans in eastern Pennsylvania. (And in his idle hours—if there ever were any such in his life—he studied foreign languages, first German and French, then Italian and Spanish.)

Franklin's printing businesses throughout the colonies prospered. In the 1740s the profits provided Franklin with such a comfortable income that in 1748, at age 42, Franklin retired from active business as a printer. At that point, he took on David Hall, a Scottish printer working in London, as a partner, paying his passage from London, and offering to pay his return if the employment did not suit him. But all worked out well. Franklin described Hall in a letter to Hall's former employer as "discrete, industrious, and honest"—in other words, much like Franklin himself. Now, in 1748, the impoverished youth who had entered Philadelphia a mere quarter of a century earlier had not only become a respected businessman, but a comparatively wealthy one as well. Retirement for Franklin did not lead to a life of quiet leisure and passive inactivity. On the contrary, retirement would only open up greater vistas for a man forever curious, forever creative. As he wrote to the New York naturalist Cadwallader Colden in 1748, now he would have "leisure to read, study, make experiments, and converse at large with such ingenuous and worthy men as are pleased to honor me with their friendship."[20]

In his Autobiography, *Franklin tells of his effort systematically to cultivate a higher standard of morality. Here is his Table of Virtues, with his brief remark on each.*

1. Temperance.
   > Eat not to Dulness.
   > Drink not to Elevation.

2. Silence.
   > Speak not but what may benefit others or your self.
   > Avoid trifling Conversation.

3. Order.
   > Let all your Things have their Places.
   > Let each Part of your Business have its Time.

4. Resolution.
   > Resolve to perform what you ought.
   > Perform without fail what you resolve.

5. Frugality.
   > Make no Expence but to do good to others or yourself: i.e.,
   > Waste nothing.

6. Industry.
   > Lose no Time. Be always employ'd in something useful.
   > Cut off all unnecessary Actions.

7. Sincerity.

> Use no hurtful Deceit.
>
> Think innocently and justly; and, if you speak, speak accordingly.

8. Justice.

> Wrong none, by doing Injuries or omitting the Benefits that are your Duty.

9. Moderation.

> Avoid Extreams.
>
> Forbear resenting Injuries so much as you think they deserve.

10. Cleanliness.

> Tolerate no Uncleanness in Body, Cloaths or Habitation.

11. Tranquility.

> Be not disturbed at Trifles, or at Accidents common or unavoidable.

12. Chastity.

> Rarely use Venery [pursuit of sexual pleasure] but for Health or Offspring; Never to Dulness, Weakness, or the Injury of your own or another's Peace or Reputation.

13. Humility.

> Imitate Jesus and Socrates.

Three

DOCTOR FRANKLIN

Hide not your Talents, they for use were made:
What's a Sun Dial in the Shade?
—*Poor Richard Improved,* 1750

BENJAMIN FRANKLIN DID FEW THINGS ALONE. HE SOUGHT INTELLECtual colleagues in Pennsylvania, then throughout the colonies, and then in the wider European world. With such companions, he could share his ideas and learn from theirs; they could stimulate one another in fuller understandings, and encourage one another to further probe the secrets of what was, after all, a fascinating universe. After the period of what Franklin called the "Drudgery of Settling new Colonies" was past, it was time for Americans to seek a higher intellectual plane.

Just such a search was the prime purpose behind his formation in 1743 of the American Philosophical Society. Franklin was using the word "philosophy" in its original sense: the love of wisdom. In the 18th century, the term "natural philosophy" was given to what later generations designated as biology, chemistry, or physics. Natural philosophers scorned such divisions even as they recognized no limits to their own serious investigations. Once again, Franklin employed the power of the printed word in his pamphlet, *Proposal for Promoting Useful Knowledge Among the British Plantations in America.*[1]

In his brief *Proposal,* Franklin laid out a vision for the society of breathtaking grandeur and breadth. All knowledge was welcome: from the propagation of trees to the preventing of disease; from the unearthing of fossils to improvements in the brewing of beer; and from new techniques in animal breeding to the surveys of land and sea, mountains and coasts, rivers and "great Roads." In short, Franklin sought to encourage a new society open to "all philosophical Experiments that let Light into the Nature of Things, tend to increase the Power of Man over Matter, and multiply the Conveniences or Pleasures of Life."

Franklin had himself, of course, taken early steps in multiplying "the Conveniences and Pleasures of Life." Knowledge, he thought, should be put to a practical, even pleasurable use. What good is a sundial in the shade? Franklin had observed the inadequacy of fireplaces to heat a room (or to warm anyone other than the person standing directly in front of it). Fireplaces not only did little to warm an entire room, they consumed an enormous amount of wood. So, applying the theoretical knowledge of heat and air currents, Franklin put forth the design of a new stove in the winter of 1740–41. The "Franklin stove," the name by which it quickly became known, gave out much more heat and consumed much less wood than a fireplace. The governor of Pennsylvania was so pleased with the new stove that he offered to give Franklin an exclusive patent to it for a period of years. But Franklin refused the offer, following a fixed principle of his: "That as we enjoy great Advantage from the Inventions of Others, we should be glad of an Opportunity to serve Others by any Invention of ours, and this we should do freely and generously."[2]

One of the tragic, and all too common, hazards of colonial city life was fire. Homes and public buildings burned, and neighbors' attempts to put out the fires generally proved too little and too late. In 1736 Franklin proposed volunteer fire companies that would gather men quickly to extinguish a blaze. Members of such a company agreed to keep leather buckets in good working order to transport water as required. They would also keep on hand large bags to assist in removing endangered goods from the flames. These volunteers agreed to meet once a month to discuss ways of improving firefighting in Philadelphia, and the small fines levied for missing a meeting would be used for the purchase of ladders, firehooks, and other instruments useful in combating a blaze.[3]

When even more men sought to join this first fire company than were needed, the group grew so large that Franklin suggested that those seeking admission form their own company elsewhere in the city. The idea caught on, and in a few years volunteer groups sprang up all over Philadelphia. "So that I question," Franklin later wrote, "whether there is a City in the World better provided with the Means of putting a Stop to beginning Conflagrations."[4]

Franklin continued to give attention to his city and to ways of making it a more comfortable place in which to live. Colonial streets, unpaved, were either dusty or muddy. The streets were sometimes so muddy that carriages bogged down to their hubs. Or when they were dry and dusty, every merchant and house-keeper found the task of keeping goods and quarters clean unending. Some householders spread gravel in front of their own doors, but this did little to mend the street as a whole. So Franklin suggested the radical idea of paving the streets, planting the notion first in his newspaper and then gathering broad support in a series of town meetings.[5]

The city soon paved its streets, lit them by gas (with an improved lamp globe design contributed by Franklin), and cleaned them on a regular schedule. Franklin was involved in so much civic improvement that when one citizen proposed the building of a hospital, potential donors held back until they learned Franklin's opinion of the project. Franklin not only approved but gave his full support in writing and worked to gain support from a reluctant assembly. By 1756 Philadelphians saw a handsome and ever more useful medical building erected in their midst.[6]

Franklin had certainly made a name for himself in his adopted hometown. But his name would soon become a familiar one throughout the Western world. And he achieved this entry onto the world stage by means of his scientific investigation into a strange phenomenon: electricity. In general, colonial Americans in the mid-18th century were seen as cultural barbarians, totally dependent for scientific progress and cultural advances upon their "betters" in England, Scotland, Holland, France, and Germany. Franklin would—almost single-handedly—change this misperception.

In 1746 Franklin attended a lecture in Boston on the subject of electricity. The lecture was part magic show and part intellectual teasing, as the lecturer demonstrated simple electrical shocks. People knew of static electricity, of course, but they had little notion of what caused it or how it could be prevented. Franklin quickly recognized that the subject needed a more systematic investigation, and he just as quickly moved to undertake it. What was the nature of this strange "fluid," and how could it be produced or controlled? Most of all, he wondered, what possible utility might electricity have for improving the welfare of humankind?

Corresponding with Peter Collinson, a Quaker merchant and scientist in London, Franklin was delighted to find another inquirer searching out this mystery of the universe. In late 1746, Collinson sent Franklin a solid-glass rod that, when rubbed rapidly with a cloth, produced an electrical charge. Franklin practiced with the tube until he could reproduce the "tricks" he had seen in Boston and had read about in reports from abroad. Soon he persuaded the local glass house to make several solid tubes, so that others could repeat the experiments and "go on the road," so to speak. One of these performers, Ebenezer Kinnersley, became especially popular, traveling up and down the Atlantic coast demonstrating some of the exciting possibilities of electricity.[7]

Soon, more equipment was needed: some jars to store the electrical charge, some wires to transmit the charge to the jars, and some sharp metal points to draw off the charge in the form of sparks, shocks, and small flames. For this new field, a new vocabulary was required—most of it provided by Franklin. The glass rod (later a sphere) became the generator, the wire the conductor, and the glass jar the condenser. The amount of electricity that this condenser could hold depended on the thickness of the glass. Holding the jar and touching the wire at the same time produced a shock, sufficient, in one experiment, to knock down six men, Franklin reported. For a special dinner in 1749, Franklin arranged to have a turkey killed by electrical shock and then roasted before a fire "kindled by the electrified bottle."[8]

In all this experimentation, theorizing, and performing, Franklin did not forget his friendly correspondent in London. Beginning in 1747, he wrote letters to Peter Collinson describing

This painting by Benjamin West dramatically re-creates Franklin's kite experiment, which proved that lightning was electricity. No experiment gave Franklin greater acclaim, either at home or abroad. *Philadelphia Museum of Art, Gift of Mr. and Mrs. Wharton Sinkler, 1958*

in great detail what he and his fellow investigators had done and with what results. One major mystery continued to haunt Franklin: namely, the exact relationship between the electricity produced in the laboratory and lightning produced in nature. Many similarities between the two phenomena could be observed, and Franklin in 1749 proceeded to list them all: both give light; the light is of similar color; in both cases the light is crooked; the motion is swift; metal serves as a conductor; a crack or noise is produced; both tear whatever they pass through; and both melt metals, destroy animals, set fire to flammable substances, and share "a sulphureous smell." Given this imposing list, it seemed highly probable that lightning was itself a form of electricity.

Franklin communicated all this to Collinson, who read the letters to the very distinguished Royal Society of London—amid much skepticism and even occasional laughter. The society's members declined to have Franklin's letters printed in their journal, but Collinson was not to be deterred. He offered the correspondence to the editor of *Gentleman's Magazine,* founded in London in 1731, who printed the letters in May 1750. Then, with additional materials, the letters were printed in London as an 86-page pamphlet titled *Experiments and Observations on Electricity Made at Philadelphia in America.* This small book was quickly translated into French, German, and Italian, even as it went through repeated editions in English.[9]

But what was the practical application of all this research for the immediate benefit of humanity? The answer: the lightning rod. Franklin had observed that metal points would attract the electricity stored in his jars, drawing if off for whatever purpose one wished. Could lightning—responsible for so many costly fires—be similarly drawn off, to run harmlessly by means of a wire into the ground? No buildings in Philadelphia were tall enough to test the theory, but Europeans tested it repeatedly and found it sound.

Then Franklin, lacking a tall building, hit upon an ingenious solution. Why not fly a kite into the storm clouds, and by means of a sharply pointed wire extended above the wood frame of the kite, draw down electricity to the earth? Or, as Franklin explained in a letter to Peter Collinson in 1752,

> And when the rain has wet the kite and twine so that it can conduct the electric fire freely, you will find it stream out plentifully from the key on the approach of your knuckle. At this key the phial [vial] may be charged; and from the electrical fire thus obtained, spirits may be kindled, and all the other electrical experiments be performed, which are usually done by the help of a rubbed globe or tube, and thereby the sameness of the electric matter with that of lightning completely demonstrated.[10]

This experiment of Franklin's needed only the artistic genius of the American painter Benjamin West to ensure the enduring image of Franklin and his kite, challenging the heavens and astounding the Western world. As the lightning rod proved ever more popular and ever more valuable, Franklin again resisted the offer to protect his invention with a patent. No, he insisted, science existed for the very purpose of benefiting humankind.[11]

In 1753 both Harvard and Yale awarded the honorary master of arts degree to the bold scientist who had never even finished high school, to say nothing of college. At this point even the Royal Society of London atoned for its earlier skepticism by granting the Copley Medal to Franklin in 1753 "on account of his curious experiments and observations on electricity"; two years later the society voted him into its exclusive membership, ruling that he would have to pay no dues. The third college in the colonies, William and Mary, likewise bestowed on Franklin the master of arts degree in 1756.

Foreign universities soon followed suit. St. Andrews University in Scotland upped the academic honors by granting him an honorary doctorate of laws. Henceforth, he was known as "Dr. Franklin." Oxford University matched St. Andrews three years later. Europe could not do enough, as country after country made him a member of its highest scientific society: Göttingen, Germany, in 1766; Paris in 1772; Edinburgh in 1774; Madrid in 1784; and St. Petersburg, Russia, in 1787. Dr. Franklin carried himself, and America with him, to the highest plateaus of international acclaim—all this based primarily on his 86-page widely read booklet.[12]

Franklin could have easily rested on all these laurels, but he was not so constituted. Ever since the founding of the American Philosophical Society in 1743 (where, incidentally, all his primitive electrical apparatus may still be seen), his scientific interests widened in ever-enlarging concentric circles. In Philadelphia such early members of the society as self-taught botanist John Bartram and distinguished astronomer David Rittenhouse brought increasing luster to the Franklin circle. But by the 1750s, he had scientific correspondents and admirers abroad. He read of their experiments with unflagging interest, even as he took time to reply to their letters and, more often than not, their questions. Franklin gave free rein to a curiosity that only grew stronger and more insistent. He would lead; he would invent. And if others beat him to the punch with an invention, he had only praise to offer.

When, for example, a French professor of "experimental philosophy" came up with a hot-air balloon in 1783, Franklin was first among the spectators and admirers. He wrote to a scientific correspondent in England, Sir Joseph Banks, president of the Royal Society and Franklin's close friend, of the great satisfaction expressed by all the witnesses. Franklin and Banks discussed the possible uses that such a balloon might have, "among which many were very extravagant." But the ever-optimistic Franklin added that this aerial experiment "may pave the way to some discoveries in natural philosophy of which at present we have no conception." This same attitude was again revealed when Franklin watched from the French side as a hot-air balloon soared across the English Channel. "What good is that?" one scorner asked. "What good is a new-born babe?" Franklin replied.[13]

His many years abroad, as well as his eight crossings of the Atlantic Ocean, gave Franklin repeated opportunities for observation, for conversation, and for intellectual stimulation. On his first crossing in 1724, when still a teenager, Franklin relieved the monotony of the trip by jumping over the side (when winds were light), swimming around the ship, and then clambering back aboard. Franklin was not only a strong swimmer but a passionate devotee of that particular form of physical activity. "The exercise of swimming," he later wrote, "is one of the most agreeable and healthy in the world." And he found that in the hottest summers in Philadelphia, if one swam for an hour or two in the evening in the Delaware River, then "one sleeps cooly the whole night."[14]

On his second sailing to London, in 1757, Franklin narrowly escaped a shipwreck that could have cost him his life. A lighthouse alerted a sleepy and negligent crew at the last minute to a threateningly near coast, so all were spared. "This Deliverance," he gratefully recalled, "impress'd me strongly with the Utility of Lighthouses, and made me resolve the building more of them in America, if I should live to return there." When someone suggested that he should build a chapel in gratitude for his survival, he replied that if he built anything, it would be another lighthouse.[15]

But in all his transatlantic crossings, he especially welcomed the opportunity to observe winds, currents, water temperatures, and more—particularly with respect to the Gulf Stream (that "river in the ocean"). Why was it, he wondered, that ships sailing from America to England made much better time (a matter of several days or even weeks) than ships making the return voyage? Also, why was it that, in sampling water temperatures in the Atlantic, he found a current where the water was noticeably warmer?

This current, the Gulf Stream, arises from the Gulf of Florida and proceeds in a northeasterly direction along the American coast at a speed of between two and four miles per hour. The current was well known to captains of whaling vessels in New England, for whales preferred to swim alongside the warmer current, though not in it. If whaling boats sailed in the Gulf Stream, while the whales swam just outside of it, they quickly lost sight of their prey. In this fashion, whales helped New England sea captains to locate, measure, and test the force of the current.

Franklin learned about the Gulf Stream from a Nantucket captain long engaged in the whaling business. American whalers navigated across the stream, never in it, to maintain their pursuit. They would see English sea captains, oblivious to the force of the stream, sailing in it, and in a day's time losing as much as 100 miles. The whalers "advised them to cross it and get out of it," the whaling captain told Franklin, "but they were too wise to be counselled by simple American fishermen," Franklin noted in a 1784 letter to Julien-David Le Roy.[16]

Franklin soon had an opportunity to put this acquired knowledge to practical use. In his capacity as postmaster general, Franklin had been consulted about the location of this current by the Board of Customs in Boston and by the Lords of the Treasury in London. And with his typical thoroughness, Franklin by 1769 was prepared to provide both offices with maps and charts, with red lines clearly delineating the Gulf Stream—to the great benefit of all future Atlantic navigation.

Other of Franklin's observations did not depend on sea travel, only on keeping his eyes open and his mind questioning. In a simple experiment, Franklin discovered around 1760 that different colors absorb heat at different rates. On a bright sunny day, one can place on the snow small squares of cloth of differing colors, ranging from solid black to pure white. After a few hours, one will observe, Franklin wrote, that the black square, absorbing much more heat, has sunk deeply into the snow, while the white piece rests lightly near the top. And, as usual, Franklin searched for the utility of this information.[17]

He found many practical applications: People should wear light clothes in the summer, darker clothes in the winter. Soldiers and sailors who must labor in the sun in the East or West Indies should have uniforms of pure white. Summer hats for all should be white. Fruit trees should be surrounded by black walls to protect the trees from frosts and to promote their growth. And "sundry other particulars of less or greater Importance," Franklin added, "will occur from time to time to attentive Minds," as he wrote in 1760 to Polly Stevenson, the daughter of his London landlady. "Attentive minds"—now there was a secret worth sharing, worth advertising.[18]

A lover of music, Franklin even concentrated his genius in that area in the early 1760s. Beginning with the common experience of producing a musical tone by passing a wet finger around the rim of a glass, Franklin then observed that many different notes could be produced with several glasses filled to various depths with water. But he wanted to produce the same sound on a more compact instrument that could be played by a single musician sitting before it, as before a harpsichord. After much experimentation, he came forth with what he called an armonica (or harmonica).

He had glasses blown in the shape of a half-sphere, each glass of a different thickness and size. A number large enough to produce

In 1761 Franklin invented the glass armonica, which consists of glass spheres of varying sizes. When the spheres are turned by a foot pedal, dampened fingers applied to the glass produce music. Long neglected, this instrument is now enjoying something of a revival as more people are learning to play it. *Franklin Collection, Yale University Library, New Haven, Conn.*

three octaves—Franklin recommended 37 to allow for some half notes as well—were turned by a common wheel or spindle. All were finely tuned, by grinding each glass as necessary. Finally, the glasses were set in a case about three feet long, tapered to accommodate the varying sizes of the glasses, from largest to smallest.

The armonica was played with both hands, as the player passed fingers around the rim of the glasses. The resulting music was "soft and plaintive," he told an Italian friend, Giambatista Beccaria, in 1762, and therefore particularly suited to Italian music. But beyond that, one should know, said Franklin, that "the advantages of this instrument are, that its tones are incomparably sweet beyond those of any other." Moreover, these tones "may be swelled or softened at pleasure by stronger or weaker pressures of the finger." Finally, "the instrument, being once well tuned, never again wants tuning."[19] European composers, including Mozart and Beethoven, wrote for it, as the armonica enjoyed a brief popularity. Over time, the fragility of the instrument discouraged its wider use.

While representing the United States in Paris in 1784, Franklin added what may at first seem a most unlikely notch on his belt of inventions: namely, daylight saving time. The prime motive in this proposal was economy, "for I love economy exceedingly," as he noted in the *Journal of Paris* in 1784. He goes on to recount, with high humor, how quite by accident he discovered that in the summer the sun rises quite early. Even more surprising, he declares with a straight face, is the fact that the sun gives light as soon as it rises. He quickly consulted the Parisian almanac, learning there that the sun would continue to rise early for weeks to come—a fact that he acknowledges would surprise others as much as himself who were not accustomed to rise before noon.

While some people assured Franklin, as he noted in the *Journal,* that the sun could not possibly be up that early, the awake and alert observer knew that he was right. He also knew that he—like so many of his friends—had generally "slept six hours longer by the light of the sun, and in exchange have lived six hours the following night by candle-light." Now, as candlelight is much more expensive than sunlight, Franklin reasoned, "my love of economy induced me to muster up what little arithmetic I was master of, and make some calculations." He calculated, assuming there were 100,000 families in Paris, they would burn unnecessarily over the summer 64,050,000 pounds of wax and tallow. This extravagant activity, he further surmised, cost the citizens of Paris the equivalent of well over $10,000 every year. And that was not economy, but folly.[20]

So what was so "scientific" about all this? Franklin, with tongue firmly in cheek, explained that his own discovery was that the sun gave off light as soon as it arose. Parisians certainly did not understand this; otherwise, they never would "have lived so long by the smoky, unwholesome, and enormously expensive light of candles, if they had really known that they might have had as much pure light of the sun for nothing."[21] However, not until laws were passed in Europe and America in the 19th and 20th centuries did daylight saving time become a staple of modern life.

As a convenience to himself, but as years passed to thousands of others as well, Franklin invented in 1785 "double spectacles," or what would soon be known as bifocals. At Parisian dinners, he found it awkward to keep changing eyeglasses from those that enabled him best to see what he was eating and those that put the faces of dinner companions across the table in clear focus. So by dividing the lens in half, with the least convex at top for closest views and the most convex at bottom for distant views, he simplified his life greatly. Now, instead of changing glasses, he only had to move his eyes up and down. Still struggling to improve his

French, he found it very helpful to be able to watch the lips of those across the table who were speaking to him, as he explained in a letter to his "Dear Old Friend" George Whatley, "so that I understand French better by the help of my spectacles."[22]

The inventiveness went on, from prescribing a treatment for gout—a painful inflammation of the joints, especially the big toe, from which Franklin suffered—to noting the advantages of travel by canal, from determining the origin of northeast storms to possible explanations for the existence of sunspots.[23] One did not have to be a genius to come up with many of Franklin's insightful explanations and observations, but one did require an "attentive mind." What prospects did the young people of Pennsylvania have for acquiring such a mind?

In 1749, when Franklin was in his mid-40s, he presented the results of his long reflection on the problems of education in his pamphlet *Proposals Relating to the Education of Youth in Pensilvania.* One point he wished to make immediately: Pennsylvania, unlike Massachusetts, Connecticut, and Virginia, had made no provision for an academy or college to "cultivate" the minds of its youth. American youth in general, Franklin observed, "are allow'd not to want [lack] Capacity; yet the best Capacities require Cultivation, it being truly with them, as with the best ground, unless well tilled and sowed with profitable Seed, produces only ranker Weeds." And as "the good Education of Youth has been esteemed by Wise Men in all Ages" to be the surest foundation for happiness among both individuals and nations, it was time for Pennsylvanians to recognize their duty—and perform it.[24]

Acknowledging the magnitude of this undertaking, Franklin aimed at getting a broad and enthusiastic number of supporters. Even with all his vigor and inspiration, Franklin knew he could not accomplish this large task alone. As was often his inclination, he would be the catalyst, the goad, the visionary. And as Thomas Jefferson would do in creating the University of Virginia, Franklin would prescribe the curriculum, determine the qualifications of the chief executive officer, discuss the diet of the students, the practical application of their studies, and so on. Unlike Jefferson, however, he did not lay out a campus or offer architectural designs for any buildings. He did win friends and support sufficient in number and means, though, to plant the seed of what would become first the College of Philadelphia, and later the University of Pennsylvania.[25]

He saw no reason why upcoming generations of Pennsylvania's youth should be reduced, as he was, to primitive programs of self-instruction and self-improvement. Let them be given the advantages that young people in other colonies already had, and let his colony take pride in its broad support of learning. And in his educational pamphlet, Franklin made clear that the end of all learning was "to serve Mankind, one's Country, Friends and Family." By the example of his life, he made that point even more clearly.

Solving the Mystery of
Lightning and Thunder

In 1767 Franklin wrote a short piece in Paris that he entitled "Of Lightning, and the Method (Now Used in America) of Securing Buildings and Persons From Its Mischievous Effects." The value of his lightning rod having already been established, Franklin now explained in simplest terms the scientific observations that led to its invention. What follows is his introduction to that work.

Experiments made in electricity first gave philosophers a suspicion that the matter of lightning was the same with the electric matter. Experiments afterwards made on lightning obtained from the clouds by pointed rods, received into bottles, and subjected to every trial, have since proved this suspicion to be perfectly well founded, and that whatever properties we find in electricity, are also the properties of lightning.

This matter of lightning, or of electricity, is an extream subtile fluid, penetrating other bodies, and subsisting in them equally diffused.

When by any operation of art or nature, there happens to be a greater proportion of this fluid in one body than in another, the body which has most, will communicate to that which has least, till the proportion becomes equal; provided the distance between them be not too great; or, if it is too great, till there be proper conductors to convey it from one to the other.

If the communication be through the air without any conductor, a bright light is seen between the bodies, and a sound is heard. In our small experiments we call this light and sound the electric spark and snap; but in the great operations of nature, the light is what we call lightning, and the sound (produced at the same time, tho' generally arriving later at our ears than the light does to our eyes) is, with its echoes, called thunder.

Four

PENNSYLVANIA POLITICS

Three may keep a secret, if two of them are dead.
—*Poor Richard's Almanack,* 1735

IN THE 18TH CENTURY, ENGLAND WAS FREQUENTLY AT WAR WITH France or Spain or both. On the frontiers of the British Empire, the colonies felt exposed—as indeed they were—to the predatory activities of France, mostly by land, or of Spain, mostly by sea. France, occupying the Mississippi Valley interior, threatened to move eastward, forging alliances with various Indian tribes. And Spain, for more than a hundred years, sailed along the Atlantic coast, probing for weaknesses on land or plunder at sea. Each colony provided for the defense of its own borders, sometimes with the assistance of the British and sometimes not. But Pennsylvania had a peculiar problem. Quakers were the earliest settlers, and even by midcentury they still constituted the ruling majority in the assembly. And Quakers were pacifists.

If military bulwarks were to be raised against the threat of foreign attack, Quakers could hardly be expected to take the lead in any armed defense. Other segments of the population, however, conscious of their colony's vulnerability, responded quickly to Franklin's 1747 pamphlet, *Plain Truth.* This work amounted to a call to arms, if only defensive arms. Four days after publishing his warning words, Franklin summoned a meeting of citizens to create "a voluntary Association of the People." Once again, Franklin would lead a large group of people where he knew they needed to go.

The public meeting was a great success. Franklin had thoughtfully printed many copies of his proposed rules for the association, with spaces for signatures as a sign of support. After the meeting, where Franklin "harangu'd them a little on the Subject," he and his helpers discovered that they had 1,200 signed copies in their hands. Then, "other Copies being dispers'd in the Country, the Subscribers amounted at length to upwards of Ten Thousand."[1]

This meant that in the space of a few weeks Franklin had pledges from able-bodied men to acquire arms, form themselves into companies, meet weekly for military instruction, and start some kind of military discipline. Women, for their part, signed separate pledges that obliged them to provide each company with its own regimental flags with colored slogans, which Franklin wrote. When the Philadelphia regiment chose Franklin as its colonel, he modestly declined on the grounds of his limited military experience. At Franklin's suggestion, another "fine Person and Man of Influence" was chosen, but Franklin remained actively involved in arranging for the defense of his colony.[2]

Philadelphia now had men and arms, but the city still needed some kind of fort or battery where cannon could be installed to fire on hostile ships coming up the Delaware River. His stalwart volunteers could hardly be expected to bear all that expense themselves. So Franklin proposed a favorite colonial fund-raising device: the lottery. Tickets were sold widely and, after some prizes had been awarded, the remaining funds were applied to the public project at hand. In the days before government bonds, monies raised in this fashion built educational facilities, governmental buildings, and even churches. So the battery was soon built, and all that was now required was some heavy artillery.[3]

Boston came through with some old cannon; these helped some, but not much. The association then wrote to England for assistance, as four emissaries of the association (including Franklin, to be sure) were dispatched to New York City to seek assistance from Governor George Clinton. The negotiations, fortunately, were conducted with liberal quantities of Madeira wine distributed to all. Clinton first refused to loan of any of New York's cannon. But after a few rounds of drinks, he offered 6. A few more drinks, and his offer was raised to 10. "And at length he very good-naturedly conceded Eighteen," Franklin reported in the *Autobiography* with much satisfaction. These "fine Cannon" were quickly transported to the Philadelphia battery, where the association posted nightly guards as long as the hostilities between England and Spain and France continued. "And among the rest," Franklin remembered, "I regularly took my Turn of Duty as a common Soldier."[4]

King George's War—as the engagement initially against Spain, then France, was called, after Britain's monarch, George II—ended in 1748, thus reducing for the moment the immediate threat of military activity in or around Pennsylvania. In fact, New Englanders more than Pennsylvanians had been directly involved in military activity in and around Nova Scotia. Franklin's role in the association had been so visible that some advisers warned him that he might be losing influence or acceptance among the pacifist Quakers, still a major segment of the colony's political leadership.

Franklin thought this unlikely, as he continued to enjoy the friendship of many Quakers. Also, during the war he published, often free of charge, arguments both for and against pacifism. He discovered, moreover, that Quakers were not all of one mind on that point. Some distinguished between a defensive war—as they considered King George's to be—and a war of aggression. Others, though rejecting the war, absented themselves from crucial votes so as not to obstruct the military effort of the association. "I afterwards estimated the Proportion of Quakers sincerely against Defense," Franklin wrote in the *Autobiography*, "as one to twenty-one only."[5]

If Quakers presented one kind of problem to Pennsylvania, Germans presented another. A sharp rise in German immigration in the 1730s created an ethnic bloc in the colony that worried many residents, including Franklin. He grew concerned that the Germans refused to learn English and seemed slow to assimilate into the majority culture. Most German communities created their own schools with both textbooks and instruction in the German language. In a long letter dated May 9, 1753, to his favorite London correspondent, Peter Collinson, Franklin concluded his observations on the Germans in Pennsylvania with uncharacteristic pessimism. If German migration is not diverted or stifled, he wrote, "they will so soon out number us, that all the advantages we have will not in My Opinion be able to preserve our language, and even our Government will become precarious."[6]

Franklin supported privately financed English schools. One explicit purpose of these schools was to Anglicize the German children. Such schools would provide the same education to German and English boys and girls, with all instruction and reading in English. On the basis of friendships formed in their early years, Franklin suggested, such children in their teenage years would intermarry, and thus solve the "German problem." Though this did not work out as early planners had hoped, years later Germans did learn English. Some of the smaller and more isolated sects, however, such as the Amish, acquired English more slowly than others. (The name of the so-called Pennsylvania Dutch is really a corruption of Pennsylvania *Deutsch,* that is, German.)

Despite his reluctance to see Germans continuing to live apart, Franklin did use his press to provide German translations of major public policies, thus keeping this important minority well informed. And he informed himself regarding their cultural patterns and overriding interests. Some of the smaller groups were pacifists, though the larger segments of their society—the Lutherans and German Reformed, for example—were not. He was impressed with one humble group, the Dunkards, or German Baptists, who held to their doctrines tenaciously, but at the same time did not believe that they had all truth in their grasp. This modesty, Franklin noted, was singular in all religious history, "every other Sect supposing itself in Possession of all Truth, and those who differ from them are so far in the Wrong."[7]

When military matters required him to go to Bethlehem, Pennsylvania, he took time to learn more about the Moravians who lived there. In Europe, this small sect was widely persecuted, causing their leaders to look for greater religious freedom in America. Franklin discovered, for example, that the majority were not pacifists, as had been commonly assumed. He knew of their communal habits: all eating together, maintaining their cattle together, males sleeping together in large dormitories, and females likewise in their separate facilities. He attended their church services and was pleased with the superior quality of music provided by violins, flutes, oboes, clarinets, and other fine instruments.

He had also heard that marriages between young men and young women were arranged by drawing lots, but he was informed that this was rarely the case. Usually, Franklin explained, "when a young Man found himself dispos'd to marry, he informed the Elders of his Class," who consulted with their counterparts in charge of the young ladies. Knowing their charges well, the elders determined if the match seemed suitable, and if so, recommended in favor of it. But if it happened that two or three young women were found to be equally suitable for the same young man, "the Lot was then recurr'd to [employed]." Franklin thought that marriages thus made would not always end up happily. True, a Moravian friend responded, but was this not also the case among the English?[8]

Franklin's leisure to investigate religious practices was sharply reduced when war between England and France broke out again in 1754. This French and Indian War, the last and most significant of the colonial wars, continued until 1763. With the threat of an alliance between French forces inland and the Iroquois Indians, the 13 colonies appeared more vulnerable than ever. To try to bring some unity to whatever military action the colonies might provide, the British Board of Trade proposed gathering a congress in Albany, New York, in 1754. Selected as one of three representatives from Pennsylvania, Franklin set out for Albany, taking time en route to draw up "A Plan for the Union of all the Colonies."[9]

Though only 7 of the 13 colonies sent representatives to Albany, all 7 voted in support of some sort of union. The plan was intended to warn France against trying to pick off the British colonies one by one: first Pennsylvania or Virginia from the west, then New York or the New England colonies from the Canadian north. But the union was also intended to increase the colonies' military effectiveness. "One principal encouragement to the French," Franklin wrote in the *Pennsylvania Gazette* on May 9, 1754, "in invading and insulting the British American dominions was their knowledge of our disunited state."

To correct that, Franklin proposed a president-general for the colonies (to be appointed by the Crown), as well as a Grand Council that could speak in their name. Everybody wants unity, Franklin somewhat sourly observed in the *Gazette*, "but when they come to the manner and form of the union, their weak noodles are perfectly distracted." Nor did the Iroquois prove any more helpful in combating the French than the colonists, as they preferred in the early stages of the war to stay strictly neutral.[10]

Although the representatives in Albany unanimously endorsed Franklin's plan, the colonial assemblies themselves, as anticipated, turned it down. At that juncture, Franklin thought the only way to get his plan going was to appeal over the heads of the assemblies to the British Parliament itself. Let Parliament do for the colonies what they seemed unwilling to do for themselves. Franklin usually shied away from giving more authority or voice to a distant Parliament in which, after all, the Americans had no representation. But if this was the only way to achieve some kind of alliance among the colonies to protect themselves against the French (and quite possibly the Indians as well), it seemed worth a try.

Parliament, however, was no more sympathetic to Franklin's plan than the colonial assemblies had been. The assemblies did not adopt it because they would be surrendering much of their authority to an unknown agency that would be placed above them.

Parliament rejected it because it seemed too democratic; that is, the people were granting power to themselves that should be reserved to the king. In the midst of this debate, Franklin created his first political cartoon: "Join, or Die." The cartoon pictured the disunited colonies as a severed snake. But outside of the Albany conference, few saw the choice as being quite that stark.[11]

To the colonial troops fighting the French in western Pennsylvania, however, the choice was quite real. In 1755 England dispatched General Edward Braddock—assisted by a young major, George Washington—with 2,500 troops to the interior (around the present site of Pittsburgh) to challenge and perhaps drive back the French. The effort did not work out well. Braddock's advance troops suffered from a surprise Indian attack and turned back in a disorganized retreat, meeting and confusing the reserve forces coming to assist them. In the battles that followed, Braddock was killed, leaving the 23-year-old Washington in charge. Some 900 British casualties resulted, giving new meaning to Franklin's "Join, or Die" declaration.[12]

In preparing for battle, Braddock had found himself critically short of wagons and supplies. He appealed to the colonists for emergency assistance, but his appeal went largely unheeded, except by Benjamin Franklin. Within a week, Franklin managed to secure 150 wagons and 259 horses, to the great gratification of General Braddock, who noted that although Virginia and Maryland had promised everything, they came through with nothing. Pennsylvania, on the other hand, had promised nothing but came through with everything. Of Franklin himself, Braddock wrote in a letter of commendation to the British Ministry: "He has executed with great punctuality and integrity [the task he voluntarily assumed], and is almost the only instance of ability and honesty I have known in these provinces. His wagons and horses," Braddock added, "are indeed my whole independence." Of course, it was not enough, but without Franklin's alert assistance, the military misadventure would have been even worse.[13]

What Franklin did, he did on his own, even pledging part of his fortune if others failed to come through. Despite his unquestionable loyalty to his colony, Franklin's relationship with Pennsylvania's governor, Robert H. Morris, deteriorated. The governor saw his role to a great extent as defender of the rights of the colony's proprietors: Pennsylvania was a proprietary colony, the land given directly by the king to its designated owners. William Penn, a Quaker, had of course been the colony's first proprietor and frequent resident there, but now in the 1750s his successors had become absentee landlords. These proprietors lived in England and rose in its social system to become conservatives in both politics and religion. Tensions between Thomas Penn, son of William, and the Pennsylvania Assembly mounted sharply when war required higher taxes and this proprietor refused to let any of his enormous land holdings in the colony be taxed.[14]

A member of the assembly since 1751, Franklin increasingly encouraged its resistance to the colony's proprietor and his extravagant claims of privilege. Thomas Penn, part of the landed classes of England, stood with them in their zealous assertion of their rights. Benjamin Franklin, in opposition, stood for and became part of the movement of the people for greater local power and greater recognition of their common rights. Conflict was inevitable between the two men, and when it came, it was accompanied by greater bitterness than either could have supposed possible.

When the Pennsylvania Assembly sought to raise £100,000 in 1756, the governor vetoed the bill on the grounds that it included a tax upon the proprietor's vast estates. The assembly was enraged. Why, in a time of great emergency, should the proprietor not join with all the colony's citizens to provide for a common defense? Members of the assembly took to the streets of Philadelphia in a demonstration against the governor and in a declaration of the true nature of their disagreement.

The stance of Thomas Penn, the members asserted, is "injurious to the Interests of the Crown, and tyrannical with Regard to the People." The rhetoric grew even stronger as the assembly demanded that the governor "give his Assent to the Bill we now present him." To demonstrate that their resolve was beyond question, they agreed to send Franklin to London as their special agent to negotiate directly with Penn.[15]

In 1757 Franklin left for England, accompanied by his 27-year-old son, William. A decade earlier, when William was still a teenager, he had joined his father on tours of inspection along the Pennsylvania frontier. He had also rendered valuable assistance in raising the required number of wagons and horses for General Braddock. Now he would again serve as his father's aide and traveling companion.

The two took up residence in the home of Mrs. Margaret Stevenson, who nursed the elder Franklin in an illness he contracted upon arrival in England. The Stevensons' daughter, Polly, grew very fond of the patient, who regarded her as a second daughter. Meanwhile, Franklin and son imitated the fashions of London, buying new clothing, new knee buckles, and appropriate stationery. "Everything about us pretty genteel," the satisfied father noted.[16]

When Thomas Penn heard that Franklin was on his way to London to negotiate face-to-face, he was not perturbed. For although Franklin might be regarded as a great man in Philadelphia, Penn noted in a 1757 letter to one Richard Peters, his "popularity is nothing here." Penn added that Franklin would be looked upon "very coldly" by the people in England who really counted. Penn even felt obliged to minimize the significance of Franklin's work with electricity. "Very few people of any consequence" have even "heard of his Electrical experiments," Penn scornfully remarked. And those who have heard of them "constitute a particular Sett of People," far removed from those who have any authority in the dispute between them.[17]

After meeting with Thomas Penn, Franklin's evaluation of his opponent was even more negative than Penn's scorn for him. Penn minimized the pledges of his father, William, disagreed about rights guaranteed in the original colonial charter, and appeared utterly unprepared to compromise on any point. For the son of William Penn, Franklin developed "a more cordial and thorough Contempt . . . than I ever felt before for any man living—a Contempt that I cannot express in Words," as he wrote to Isaac Norris in 1758. Such strong sentiments on both sides did not promise much in the way of fruitful negotiations on their deep-seated dispute. Yet Franklin remained in London until 1762, hoping for some sort of breakthrough.[18]

When none came, Franklin concluded that the whole matter of a colony owned by an absentee landlord (as a trustee for the king) ought to be reconsidered. And as much as he disliked the notion of Pennsylvania becoming a royal colony like Virginia and New York, he hoped the king might prove to be a better "landlord" than the arrogant rascal sitting in London jealously guarding his great wealth and proud privileges. At this time, Franklin thought that the only choice for Pennsylvania was between a proprietor and the king. But before many years had passed, a third—

and far more radical—option arose. That option was nothing less than independence.

After a time, Penn refused even to meet with Franklin, forcing him to meet with his attorney instead. Likewise, Franklin refused to be kept waiting for concessions that never came. And so he decided to spend his time in more profitable, or at the very least more pleasant, diversions. He renewed old friendships in London, and made many new friends, including the Scottish philosopher and historian David Hume and the chemist and Unitarian Joseph Priestley. But these friends were only part of the "particular Sett" that, in Penn's view, presented no challenge to his position and authority.

However, some events in the colony did challenge Penn's authority, and Franklin seized every opportunity to side against him. For example, Franklin took the part of the Delaware Indians against Penn, whom the Indians charged with fraudulent land deals. The proprietor purchased some lands from the Delawares, but stole more. Franklin, along with many Quakers, backed the Delawares in their protests against Penn. But the king and his advisers backed the proprietor, seeing the colonies in general and Franklin in particular as pushing too hard for the right to make decisions that must be reserved to the Crown.[19]

Franklin saw the Pennsylvania Assembly as analogous to Britain's House of Commons so far as authority over their own colony was concerned. But the authorities in England did not share that view. Of course, Parliament could legislate for England, but they believed it could legislate for the colonies as well. And all legislation passed by the colonies was subject to royal review and rejection.

Franklin no longer believed that he could play the proprietor off against the king. They were in league together to cramp and suppress every colonial step, however tentative, toward self-rule. Franklin had struck out with Penn; now he was striking out with Parliament and the Crown. Not much remained for him to do in London. So with his son, William, he toured northern England and Scotland in late 1759, and in 1761, with William again as a traveling companion, he toured the Netherlands. The pair returned to England in time to see King George III crowned as the new monarch in September 1761. By summer of the following year, leaving William behind, Franklin boarded a ship bound for Philadelphia. While he was en route to America, William was married, and shortly afterward appointed royal governor of New Jersey. In the five years in London, from 1757 to 1762, the son fared better than his father did so far as concrete achievements were concerned.[20]

In his absence, Franklin had been elected every year to the Pennsylvania Assembly, even though he attended none of its sessions. Now, back in residence, he was in 1764 elected Speaker of that restless body. Meanwhile, the French and Indian War had finally ground to an end, with Britain the victor. By the terms of the 1763 Peace of Paris, France ceded all of Canada to Britain, along with its many claims to lands east of the Mississippi River. As for that great river itself, Britain won full navigation rights all the way to its mouth in New Orleans. Spain, having joined France in 1761, paid the price of choosing the wrong side by losing Florida, but—by a secret agreement with France—it won New Orleans and Louisiana.

The settlement was certainly more than England could have hoped for, as the French Empire in the New World was reduced to fishing rights off Newfoundland and two small islands in the Gulf of St. Lawrence. Such a generous windfall, one might suppose, would greatly improve relations between England and its colonies. The opposite happened. The long war cost England's treasury dearly. Meanwhile, the colonies benefited markedly from the final terms of peace; consequently, Parliament said the colonies should help pay for that costly war.

The normal method of raising money from the colonies was for the royal advisers to send a request to the colonial governors, who would in turn present the request to their local legislative assemblies. After discussion, debate, and some ill-tempered grumbling, the assemblies would meet most if not all the royal requests. This time, however, Parliament decided to do things differently. It levied a tax directly on the colonies by means of a Stamp Act, leaving the local assemblies out of the picture completely. By terms of this proposed act, virtually every printed piece of paper in the colonies would be taxed: deeds, almanacs, newspapers, advertisements, and countless certificates of compliance to demonstrate that customs regulations were being obeyed. The Stamp Act would constitute a daily reminder of royal prerogative, a daily irritant in every relationship between the colonies and the motherland.[21]

Franklin at first did not see the full implications of the Stamp Act, even though mobs in Philadelphia—angry at his passivity—attacked his house, which Deborah hurried to defend. Still preoccupied with the indignities he suffered at the hands of the Penns in London, he thought that royal protection was the prudent way to go. On this occasion, he badly misjudged public opinion, as protests up and down the Atlantic coast grew louder and more radical. Franklin still hoped for some mediation, some compromise. But neither Parliament nor the colonial governments were thinking of compromise. Somebody had to back down. Parliament declined to do so, and in February 1765, despite many warnings, it passed the much-condemned Stamp Act.

Franklin by this time was back in London, as agent for the colony of Pennsylvania and soon other colonies as well. With other colonial agents, he met with the prime minister, George Grenville, in early February in an effort to delay or derail the passing of the act. But to no avail. After the act passed, Franklin soon heard of the strength and unity of colonial protests. What the Albany Plan of Union failed to accomplish in 1754, the Stamp Act managed to achieve almost in an instant: namely, colonial unity.

Mob violence erupted in Boston, New York City, and Philadelphia. Men who called themselves Sons of Liberty threatened to take the law into their own hands, and public outcries tumbled over each other in an effort to be heard. Franklin's old printing partner, David Hall, summed it up for his friend in a letter dated September 6, 1765: "There seems to be a general Discontent all over the Continent with that Law, and many thinking their Liberties and Privileges as English Men lost, or at least in great Danger, seem Desperate."[22]

Franklin was a bit desperate, too, as critics from home questioned his loyalty, his patriotism, and above all his diligence as colonial agent for failing to prevent the passage of the Stamp Act. But now, after the dreaded deed was done, Franklin wasted no time in lobbying for the suspension, if not the outright repeal, of the despised act. If articles or letters unfriendly to the American cause appeared in the London press, Franklin tried to answer every one, often anonymously. He met with members of Parliament as frequently and repeatedly as possible, many of them confessing to a surprising ignorance of American affairs.

In October 1765, a Stamp Act Congress met in New York City and demanded that there be no taxation of the colonists by a body in which they had no voice, no representation. But Parliament felt even more pressure to repeal the act from British merchants who suffered severely from boycotts that several colonies imposed on all goods of British manufacture. Late in 1765, a group of British merchants lobbied Parliament to recognize Franklin as *the* authentic American voice in London so that he could convince Parliament to repeal the Stamp Act. In February of the next year, he addressed a committee of the whole of the House of Commons, and responded to nearly 200 questions with abundant patience, good judgment, and sweet reason.

When the committee asked what was the temper of America toward Great Britain before the end of the French and Indian War, Franklin responded that the colonists willingly obeyed the laws of Parliament and the directives of the king. Britain needed no garrisons or forts to keep the colonists in line, he asserted. "They were led by a thread." But in the last two years, he said in his testimony before the House in February of 1766, Britain had moved from gentle guidance to dictatorial direction. And Americans "think it extremely hard and unjust, that a body of men, in which they have no representatives" should give and grant what is not theirs to give. With increasing pressure from home and abroad, and following a change in the leading ministers of the government, Parliament, in February 1766, repealed the Stamp Act—though the vote was by no means unanimous. Franklin gave some credit to luck, or, as he said, to what the "Pious" would call "Providence."[23]

Following the repeal, Franklin became the strongest voice in England for colonial interests, officially for Georgia in 1768, for New Jersey in 1769, and Massachusetts in 1770, as well as of course Pennsylvania—but unofficially for all. He wrote articles, answered letters, lobbied without ceasing for an American cause of greater latitude that at the time he thought was also Britain's cause. But the interests of these two parties soon diverged.

Can the American Colonies Possibly Unite?

In 1754 Franklin tried desperately to convince the colonies that they needed to join together for mutual defense against the French along the western frontier. Though he failed in this effort, the earnestness of his attempt is evident in the paragraph below, as well as in his first political cartoon—both published in the Pennsylvania Gazette *of May 9, 1754.*

The Confidence of the French in this Undertaking [building forts and making alliances with the Indians] seems well grounded on the present disunited State of the British Colonies, and the extreme Difficulty of bring-

Library of Congress, Washington, D.C.

ing so many different Governments and Assemblies to agree in any speedy and effectual Measures for our common Defence and Security; while our Enemies have the very great Advantage of being under one Direction, with one Council, and one Purse. Hence, and from the great distance of Britain, they presume that they may with Impunity violate the most solemn Treaties subsisting between the two Crowns, kill, seize and imprison our Traders, and confiscate their Effects at Pleasure (as they have done for several Years past), murder and scalp our Farmers, with their Wives and Children, and take an easy Possession of such Parts of the British Territory as they find most convenient for them; which if they are permitted to do, must end in the Destruction of the British Interest, Trade and Plantations in America.

Five

THE ROAD TO SEPARATION

He that lieth down with dogs, shall rise up with fleas.
—*Poor Richard's Almanack,* 1733

IN HIS EARLIER STAY IN LONDON, FRANKLIN HAD LABORED—
without any happy results—to reach agreement with the proprietor, Thomas Penn. Now, in the decade from 1765 to 1775, he had to contend with both Parliament and the king (and with Penn, too, on occasion). His voice in these critical years was still the only American voice that could be heard in the clamorous debates, but it was a voice often unheeded, and now and then ridiculed. In the furor over the Stamp Act and its repeal, one might suppose that the American point of view was well understood, perhaps even accepted. But as Franklin quickly learned, this was not so. The case had to be made over and over, and any permanent advances were difficult to detect.

By 1767 Franklin seized his favorite weapon, the pen, to explain as carefully and coolly as he could why Americans should not be directly taxed by the English Parliament. In an article entitled "On the Propriety of Taxing America," Franklin took up the most common arguments put forward by Parliament, then refuted each one in turn. For example, Parliament repeatedly asserted that the colonies were settled at its expense. Not true, replied Franklin. He reminded readers of the early histories of Virginia, Massachusetts, New York, and Pennsylvania. These colonies were founded without direct support from England. Only in the case of Georgia and Nova Scotia did Parliament play a direct role in settling the colonies.

Or again, Parliament argued that the colonies received their constitutions from that legislative body, and that Parliament therefore would certainly not surrender its right to tax. No; colonial charters came directly from the king, Franklin pointed out. Further, it was widely believed, in Parliament and out, that the colonists were "protected from the Indians at the expense of Parliament." Show us the records, Franklin demanded. The fact is "that they protected themselves, at their own expense, for near 150 years after the first settlement." Applying to Parliament for aid against the Indians would never have occurred to any of the colonies, as that body's neglect of the colonies was notorious.

Then the British argued that the colonists were the chief beneficiaries of the French and Indian War. True, Franklin conceded, a lot of land in North America fell into British hands, but this land was "ceded not to the colonies, but to the crown, which is now granting it away in large tracts to British gentlemen." Many British officials also asserted that the colonies paid no taxes. What nonsense, Franklin exploded. "They have their own civil and military establishments to support," and taxes are heavy.

Finally, some leaders in the British government offered the absurd argument that the colonists denied that Parliament had any authority over them. On the contrary, Franklin argued, the colonists have accepted Parliamentary acts designed to regulate trade, along with many other applications of English law to colonial situations. On one point and one point only do they deny the authority of Parliament over them: namely, "the right to raise money upon the colonies by internal taxes." This was and remained the nub of the dispute between the colonies and Britain.[1]

But was anybody listening? Was anybody willing to return to the patterns of governing that prevailed before 1763? Could anybody understand what so suddenly had gone sour? As Franklin explained to Lord H. H. Kames in 1767, the affection for Britain in the colonies was still strong, so strong that the British rulers, if wise, could easily govern the colonies without force and at little expense for years to come. "But," Franklin lamented, "I do not see here a sufficient quantity of the wisdom that is necessary to produce such a [result], and I lament the want [lack] of it."[2]

If in his 1767 tract he disposed of arguments commonly offered on behalf of Parliament, in 1768 he tried to explain "The Causes of the American Discontents." In an effort to try to make the American position more palatable to the British, he simply presented it as though he were a disinterested observer. He first reviewed the traditional method of raising money from the colonies that had prevailed before 1768.

The Crown or one of the high officers in the British government would send letters to the colonial governors, explaining the reasons for the request for funds or troops. Then Britain would rely "on their prudence, duty and affection to his Majesty's Government, that they would grant such sums, or raise such numbers of men, as were suitable to their respective circumstances." And who knew those "respective circumstances" better than a local legislature, Franklin asked. Certainly not a government 3,000 miles away. But, the best argument of all for maintaining this pattern was that it had worked for many years—worked without inciting rebellion or deep distrust.

It was also well known, Franklin pointed out, that the right to tax their own citizens "was essential to English liberty." It was essential in England, for only the House of Commons could levy taxes and solicit funds. If the assemblies in America were to their colonies as the House of Commons was to England, then similar rights should be conceded to each assembly. The British officials who departed from this time-honored assumption must have known that—as was the case with the Stamp Act—it would give "great Offense."

Their action was not one of ignorance, Franklin argued, but of malice. The simultaneous passing of a Quartering Act, which required colonists to house British soldiers in their homes, only inflamed the Americans more. If soldiers had to be dispatched to enforce the Stamp Act, that should suggest (to any who were sufficiently wise) that something was fundamentally wrong with the act itself.[3]

New York had taken the lead in opposing the Quartering Act, so that Parliament responded with another law that specified that New York would not have the right to pass any laws until it complied. This raised fears in all the other colonies that their broadest freedoms were threatened. The message seemed to be, in Franklin's words, "Obey implicitly laws made by Parliament of Great Britain, to force money from you without your consent, or you shall enjoy no rights or privileges at all."

Meanwhile, Britain tightened custom regulations and appointed its own governors to enforce them. As to the governors themselves, "they are," Franklin wrote (in "Causes of American Discontents"), "generally strangers to the Provinces they are sent to govern." Moreover, they left their families behind when they came to America, as their single purpose was to make money as fast as they could, then return to England. "Frequently men of vicious characters and broken fortunes," Franklin complained, were dispatched to America, as one wishes to get rid of a bad penny. And when these unsavory governors finally left America, Franklin noted, they "care[d] not what is said or thought of them after they are gone." Was it any surprise that there were "discontents" among the colonists?[4]

But Britain was not satisfied with extortion by taxation or with saddling America with corrupt officials. It wished to cramp and stifle American manufacturing. Britain required all raw materials produced in the colonies to be sent back to England (at great expense), manufactured into a finished product there, then shipped back to America (at great expense again). The colonists finally purchased these goods at unnecessarily inflated prices. The final insult was that England along with Scotland emptied their jails in order to send "rogues and villains" to the colonial settlements. How nice of them! Perhaps, said Franklin, the colonies should return the favor by exporting rattlesnakes to their cities.[5]

The Americans had many reasons to explain the current ill humor between those on one side of the ocean and those on the other. Franklin would not expect Englishmen to be persuaded by any of these contentions, but if anybody really wanted to understand what Americans were actually thinking, he would do his best to assist them in that effort. On the other hand, Britons did think that the repeal of the Stamp Act might have left Americans with a false sense of a Parliamentary retreat. To reassert its authority, Parliament accompanied the repeal of the Stamp Act with the Declaratory Act, which boldly proclaimed its right to legislate for the colonies "in all cases whatsoever." Perhaps a few pieces of legislation might remind the colonists of that claim.

The House of Lords protested the repeal as an unwise capitulation, and the House of Commons ruled that the colonies should at least cover the cost of all those stamps that were never used. And then Parliament passed a whole list of new taxes on such items as lead, paint, glass, and tea. These Townshend duties (named after the new chancellor of the Exchequer, Charles Townshend) were sure to keep colonial resentments at a peak of passion, for what did the Stamp Act repeal mean after all? Not much, it seemed. Franklin conceded that the empire could control commerce, as long as it benefited the whole empire, rather than offering a small advantage to one part and great injury of another. But what would not work, Franklin asserted, was Britain's ill-advised effort to tax one part of its empire to the point of the colonists' desperation and sullen resentment.

In 1767 and 1768 Franklin still saw the unity of the British Empire as something to be protected and cherished. That empire was like a "fine and noble Chinese vase," Franklin wrote to Lord Richard Howe in July 1776, that should not be chipped away at, but held as a precious whole. And in those years, he assured the prime minister and others that Americans did not desire independence, but only a clear understanding that Parliamentary laws could be applied to the colonies only with the latter's assent. "The people of G. Britain are Subjects of the King," Franklin agreed, but the "Parliament has Power only within the Realm." If the colonial verbal assault could be aimed at Parliament alone, and not the king, Franklin hoped that the fragile vase could be preserved.[6]

Meanwhile, family news—always slow to arrive across the Atlantic—cheered him with word of his daughter Sarah's marriage to a Philadelphia merchant, Richard Bache, in 1767. A later ship brought more distressing news: his wife, Deborah, had suffered a stroke from which she never fully recovered. Affecting her both mentally and physically, the stroke interrupted the long and affectionate correspondence between husband and wife. Just a year earlier, Franklin had written to his "Debbie" that the repeal of the Stamp Act made it possible for him to send her a new gown, because the boycott on British goods was lifted after the repeal. But if that boycott had never been lifted, then, Franklin wrote, he would take pride in having been clothed "from head to foot in woolen and linen of my wife's manufacture," and "I never was prouder of any dress in my life."[7]

Correspondence of a very different sort widened the breach between Franklin and British authorities and, for a time, subjected Franklin to a possible charge of treason. These letters, written between 1767 and 1769, were from the governor and lieutenant governor of Massachusetts (Thomas Hutchinson and Andrew Oliver, respectively) to Thomas Whately, former undersecretary of the Treasury in London. New England was still on the edge of rebellion, they wrote, and without a strong British hand, the region "will soon and forever be in perpetual anarchy and disobedience." There must be, Hutchinson wrote early in 1769, "an abridgment of what are called English liberties." This correspondence somehow fell into Franklin's hands. The sentiments contained in the letters only confirmed his suspicions of double-dealing by certain colonial authorities.

Franklin took a drastic step: he made the correspondence public to the great embarrassment of both Hutchinson and Oliver

(Whately had died), and to the endangerment of Franklin's personal safety in London. Franklin, reasonably sure that his own mail—especially that from friends in Massachusetts—had been opened, could ease his conscience for his intemperate action. He sent the incriminating letters to Thomas Cushing, Speaker of the House of Representatives in Massachusetts. He told Cushing that he was less inclined to blame Parliament for the current situation, seeing that the advice to tax and restrain Americans had—at least in this instance—come from some Americans themselves. When the contents of the letters became widely known in Massachusetts, the public stir exceeded anything that Franklin had anticipated. As Franklin said of Hutchinson and Oliver, in trying to prevent a revolution they had provoked one.

Governor Hutchinson managed to obtain a copy of Franklin's letter to Speaker Cushing—colonial mails were not all that secure—and promptly turned it over to Lord William Dartmouth, one of the king's ministers. Dartmouth found Franklin's letter treasonous, and urged General Thomas Gage, head of Britain's military forces in America, to obtain the original of the letter so that Franklin could be brought to justice. Gage failed to locate the original; in all probability Cushing had wisely destroyed it after making a copy for himself. So Franklin avoided a trial, but not the scorn of several of the king's advisers.[8]

In the midst of all the political shenanigans on both sides of the Atlantic, Franklin somehow had time to give attention to a subject he had long neglected: slavery. He had not neglected the issue of education for African Americans. As early as the 1740s, the preacher George Whitefield, who founded an orphanage in Bethesda, Georgia, helped call Franklin's attention to the sad fact that education for the large slave population was much neglected in all the colonies. An English philanthropic organization, Dr. Bray's Associates, also took the education and religious conversion of blacks under its wing. Involved like Whitefield in the early settlement of Georgia, the associates invited Franklin to join them in their efforts, which he quickly did.

In a 1763 letter to John Waring in London, Franklin indicated that in a visit to the Philadelphia Charity School he was much impressed by the natural capacities of the black students. "Their Apprehension seems as quick," Franklin wrote, "their Memory as strong, and their Docility equal in every respect to that of white Children." So why should this be such a great surprise? Franklin confessed that he had earlier entertained a different view of African Americans, then added: "I will not undertake to justify all my Prejudices, nor to account for them." Like many in the 18th century—or later centuries—Franklin's consciousness in this area was only slowly raised.[9]

But by 1772 he was ready to rethink the legitimacy of the pervasive institution of slavery and to set free his own two slaves. He also questioned Britain's role in promoting the slave trade. In a letter that year to an antislavery Quaker friend, he wrote of "the Hypocrisy of this Country [Great Britain] which encourages such a detestable Commerce." On the one hand, Franklin argued, Britain prides itself upon its "Love of Liberty," but on the other it encourages and supports and profits from the exploited labors of thousands of slaves. Franklin added, a bit prematurely, "I am glad to hear that the Disposition against keeping Negroes grows more general in North America."[10]

British courts managed to free a single black man who had accidentally landed in England, but, wrote Franklin in 1772 in a letter to the *London Chronicle,* "it is to be wished that the same humanity may extend itself among numbers." And if freedom for the millions of slaves seemed beyond the realm of possibility, he continued, it should at the very least be possible "to obtain a law for abolishing the African commerce in slaves, and declaring the children of present slaves free after they become of age." About 100,000 new slaves were imported annually to the British colonies, but about one-third of these died before they reached American shores or died soon thereafter from illnesses contracted aboard ship.

To what purpose, Franklin wondered. Some said people should remember the rice and sugar that these slaves produced for others' consumption, but the scales did not balance, Franklin noted. "Can the sweetening of our tea, &c. with sugar be a circumstance of such absolute necessity?" Can it be compared in any way to the "misery produced among our fellow creatures, and such a constant butchery of the human species by this pestilential detestable traffic in the bodies and souls of men?"[11] These passionate words suggest more than a frivolous thought momentarily entertained by Franklin. Indeed, when Franklin returned to Philadelphia in 1775, he joined the Quaker-founded abolitionist society there, later even accepting its presidency.

Meanwhile, there was politics. Franklin had tried in virtually every way he knew how to change the views of king, royal boards and councils, and Parliament. And possibly, if luck or Providence were on his side, he might even alter English public opinion. He had many arrows in his quiver, but there was one he had not yet employed in these years of rising tensions: namely, satire. In 1773, therefore, he composed *Rules by Which a Great Empire May Be Reduced to a Small One.*

One such rule, he noted, was this: as "the Possibility of Separation may always exist, take special Care the Provinces are never incorporated with the Mother Country, that they do not enjoy the same Common Rights, the same Privileges in Commerce" as the parent. This, he suggested, would certainly endear the children to their benevolent parents. Or another rule: when the colonies prospered, grew in strength, and purchased more and more British goods, Britain should "resent it as if they had done you Injury."

Rule number six specified that no matter how peaceable the colonies had been for many decades, the Great Empire should always treat them as rebellious or about to become so. And in appointing royal governors or other royal officials, England should always choose those who are "ignorant, wrong-headed, and insolent." In that way, Franklin suggested, the people would surely conclude that the king who appointed them was likewise ignorant, wrong-headed, and insolent. If it became necessary for the colonists to sue for the correction of injustice, another rule stated, the English should be sure to "punish the Suitors with long Delay, enormous Expense, and a Final Judgment in favor of the Oppressor." Slowly but surely, in this fashion the colonists would come to think of all royal government as "detestable." And so through a list of 20 rules, Franklin in biting satire offered his "advice" on how to reduce a great empire to a pathetic remnant.[12]

But in 1773 Britain was in no mood for satire, only obedience. As for Benjamin Franklin, it was time to bring that arrogant agent and stinging pest to his knees. It was time for him to experience humiliation and abuse, taunts and ridicule. The next year, 1774, Franklin was summoned to appear before the Privy Council, the body of advisers closest to the king, to answer specific charges that hinted at treason against His Majesty. But in the vitriolic attack that followed, Franklin's enemies ranged far and wide in their accusations so that Franklin would appear to be the chief conspirator, agitator, and enemy of Britain.

His principal antagonist, Alexander Wedderburn, the solicitor general of England, warmed to his task as the hour-long interrogation of Franklin continued. The lonely colonial agent did have some friends in the room (both English and American), but they were permitted no part in the proceedings. Franklin stood alone, without lawyers, without files or folders, without any notes or papers of his own.[13] Everything, already bad, grew suddenly worse when news of the Boston Tea Party reached London.

The Townshend duties had all been cancelled—except for the tax on tea. Would that be enough to mollify the Americans? Apparently not. When several ships loaded with tea sailed into Boston Harbor late in 1773, aroused Bostonians refused to let the ships be unloaded and the merchandise sold. On December 16, some 5,000 agitated citizens gathered in Old South Church to determine their next course of action. Late that night, many citizens, some disguised as Indians, boarded three ships and threw their entire cargoes of tea into the salty waters. A very pleased John Adams wrote in his diary the next day: "This destruction of the tea is so bold, so daring, so firm, intrepid and inflexible, and it must have so important consequences." And so it did—for England, for Massachusetts, and for Franklin.[14]

But Franklin was a Philadelphian, not a Bostonian. What did that "intrepid" Tea Party have to do with him? How could he be held accountable in any way? In calm and dispassionate times, he could not be held accountable. But these were times of rising heat and great passions. Franklin was responsible, English authorities confidently asserted, because his real aim was to become governor of Massachusetts. That was why, they reasoned, he campaigned so vigorously and underhandedly against the current governor, Thomas Hutchinson.

It was a sham argument, of course, but it seemed enough to justify even more vitriol heaped upon Franklin as he stood before the Privy Council. Wedderburn denounced the Philadelphian as "the true incendiary" behind every American agitation. Becoming governor of Massachusetts was only a first step to his becoming the tyrannical head of a "Great American Republic." Indeed, Franklin, Wedderburn suggested, was already acting not as a mere colonial agent, but as a minister of a "foreign independent state." Wedderburn concluded in a burst of extravagant oratory: "I hope, my lords, you will mark and brand this man, for the honour of this country, of Europe, and of mankind." Franklin deserved no mercy, no forgiveness: "He has forfeited all the respect of societies and men."[15]

So how did Franklin respond to this avalanche of abuse? With silence. He said nothing, whether from the sense that his words would make absolutely no difference, or from his furious contempt for those vilifying him. Later in correspondence, however, he had much to say, and his tone was unforgiving. He now referred to England as "this old rotten state" and its ministers as the very embodiment of "extreme corruption." Why should the colonies any longer consider union with Britain as a great good to be pursued, he wondered. "I apprehend, therefore," he wrote to Joseph Galloway, a Philadelphia friend, on February 25, 1775, "that to unite us intimately will only be to corrupt and poison us also."[16]

To Charles Thomson, another Philadelphia friend, Franklin wrote four days after his "trial" that those who berated him had the nerve to claim "sovereignty over three millions of virtuous, sensible people in America," but in fact "appeared to have scarce discretion enough to govern a herd of swine." These strong words came from a man of gentle wit who usually practiced conciliation and compromise.[17] But not after his humiliating experience before the Privy Council in January 1774. Little remained for him to do in London.

The Privy Council, however, was not through with Franklin. Its members fired Franklin as deputy postmaster general, and described his petition for the removal of Governor Hutchinson as "groundless, vexatious, and scandalous." Then they turned to Parliament to deal with the rebellious Bostonians. Parliament passed a series of laws known as the Coercive Acts, or in American history as the Intolerable Acts. These acts closed the port of Boston to all commerce and required its citizens to reimburse the East India Company for all the tea that had been destroyed and the government for all the taxes that would have been collected on it. British troops would once again be housed and fed in local homes. Boston citizens who were arrested would be transported to Canada to ensure a "fair trial," and the powers of the royal governor would be greatly expanded. The British theory was that by these actions Boston would be isolated from all the other colonies; the American reality was that all the other colonies regarded Boston's mistreatment as their own.

In Philadelphia, effigies of Wedderburn and Hutchinson were paraded through the streets and then burned—by an electrical spark. More significantly, the First Continental Congress gathered in Philadelphia in the fall of 1774. Samuel Adams, cousin of John and chief propagandist in New England, saw the calling of this Congress as a step in the right direction and an appropriate response to his earlier denunciations of British actions. "With what resentment and indignation," he wrote in the *Boston Gazette* in

1771, "did we first receive the intelligence of a design to make us tributary, not to natural enemies, but infinitely more humiliating, to fellow subjects!" His rhetoric rising, he added: "And yet, with unparalleled insolence, we are told to be quiet when we see that very money which is torn from us by lawless force made use of still further to oppose us, to feed and pamper a set of infamous wretches who swarm like the locusts of Egypt."[18] The Congress, meeting for seven weeks, again imposed strict limits on the importation of goods of British manufacture. More ominously, that body also recommended that every colony arm itself and prepare its militia for whatever might lie ahead.

In February 1775, both houses of Parliament officially declared Massachusetts to be in a state of rebellion. In March, Franklin, after ten increasingly difficult years in England, left for America. His last days in England were spent answering questions from friends about America and what the current sentiments were. "Members of both Houses of Parliament [called] to inform me what passed in the Houses, and discourse with me on the debates and on motions made or to be made." In his "Account of Negotiations in London," Franklin added that London merchants dropped by to express their concerns about the boycotts and about keeping American ports open. Quakers came by to express their anxieties—so much busyness that the harried, hurried Franklin could only admit that he "had no time to take notes on almost anything."[19]

He initially doubted that he could get everything done before his scheduled sailing date of March 21, but he and his 15-year-old grandson, Temple Franklin (son of William), did manage to climb aboard with luggage, official papers, and informal messages for friends in Philadelphia. Young Temple had been sent to England to attend school outside of London, but he regularly spent his vacation periods with his grandfather in town, and the bond between them grew close.[20]

Franklin spent the first half of the six-week voyage recording his version of the recent bruising events in England, the second half of the voyage studying the Gulf Stream once more, taking the ocean's temperatures from two to four times a day. While Franklin and grandson were sailing in unusually good April weather, unplanned military actions in Lexington and Concord, Massachusetts, determined America's destiny in ways that not even Franklin had foreseen. On May 5, Franklin's ship docked at the foot of Market Street in Philadelphia.

On August 18, 1768, Franklin published in the London
Chronicle *a series of "Queries" designed to make the American case against direct taxation of the colonies by Parliament, especially in the minds of "those Gentlemen who are for vigorous Measures against the Americans."*

1. Have the Colonists refused to answer any reasonable requisitions made to their Assemblies by the Mother Country?
2. If they have not refused to grant reasonable aids in the way which they think consistent with liberty, why must they be stripped of their property without their own consent, and in a way which they think inconsistent with liberty?
3. What is it for a people to be enslaved and tributary, if it be not [this]: To be forced to give up their property at the arbitrary pleasure of persons, to whose authority they have not submitted themselves, nor chosen for the purpose of imposing taxes upon them? . . .
4. Has not the British Parliament, by repealing the stamp act, acknowledged that they judged it improper? Is there any difference between the stamp act, and the act obliging the Americans to pay whatever we [the British] please for articles which they cannot do without, as glass and paper? . . .

5. If that be true, which is commonly said, That the Mother Country gains two millions [pounds sterling] a year by the Colonies, would it not have been wiser to have gone on quietly in the happy way we were in, till our gains by those rising and flourishing countries [colonies] should amount to three, four, or five millions a year, than by these new-fashioned vigorous measures to kill the goose which lays the golden eggs? Would it not have been better policy, instead of taxing our Colonists, to have done whatever we could to enrich, and encourage them to take off our articles of luxury, on which we may put our own price, and thus draw them into paying us a voluntary tax; than deluge them in blood, thin their countries, impoverish and distress them, interrupt their commerce, force them on bankruptcy, by which our merchants must be ruined, or tempt them to emigrations, or alliances with our enemies?

6. The late [French and Indian] war could not have been carried on without America, nor without Scotland? Have we treated America and Scotland in such a manner as is likely in future wars to encourage their zeal for the common cause? ...

7. Are not the subjects of Britain concerned to check a ministry, who, by this rage of heaping taxes on taxes, are only drawing into their own hands more and more wealth and power, while they are hurting the commercial interests of the empire as a whole?

Six

W AR AND PEACE

Happy that Nation—fortunate that age—whose history is not
diverting.   —*Poor Richard's Almanack,* 1740

A NEWSPAPER "EXTRA" ON MAY 6, 1775, ANNOUNCED FRANKLIN'S
arrival in Philadelphia the day before. "Dr. Franklin," the paper
reported, "is highly pleased to find us arming and preparing for
the worst events." The bulletin then added, "He thinks nothing
else can save us from the most abject slavery and destruction; at
the same time [he] encourages us to believe a spirited opposition
will be the means of our salvation."[1] So Franklin found his return
much anticipated and keenly observed. He also found it good to
be home, though "home" would never be the same, as his wife,
Deborah, had passed away six months before.

Franklin had much to tell his fellow citizens about the political
atmosphere in Great Britain, but his news would have to wait, for
Philadelphians had much to tell him. Their news concerned events

in Massachusetts—events that pronounced an American Revolution already under way. What had happened while he was crossing the ocean, his friends and neighbors hurried to say, was this: On April 19 British troops, at the direction of General Thomas Gage, were ordered to march to Concord to destroy an ammunition dump reported to be there. Soldiers were directed to destroy all guns or artillery, to dump any gunpowder out of its barrels into the Concord River, and to put lead musket balls in their pockets and throw them little by little into ponds, ditches, and so on. All this was to be done in the early morning hours of the 19th, preferably while the Yankees were still in bed.

The military orders called for great dispatch and great secrecy, but neither condition was maintained. The British troops, some 700 or 800 of them, were slow to get started, slower to get themselves organized and underway. As for secrecy, this was virtually impossible to maintain, as Bostonians kept their eyes and ears open for any unusual activity. Besides, a silversmith named Paul Revere rode in great haste into the countryside to warn that the British were coming. On the way to Concord, the king's army came to Lexington (about eight or nine miles from Cambridge, their point of departure), and there confronted some 60 or 70 local militiamen gathered on the green. Neither side was quite sure what to do. The British had orders only to destroy the ammunition stored in Concord. On the other hand, they could hardly ignore the presence of an armed enemy, poised to do what? The militiamen, on their part, had earlier agreed not to "meddle" with the British "unless they should insult us," in the words of Captain John Parker.

After some deliberation, the British decided to disarm the locals, then march on to Concord. In the confusion and maneuvering, a shot was fired, quickly followed by many other shots from both sides. After 15 or 20 minutes, when the smoke cleared, four Americans lay dead on Lexington Green, and four others were killed nearby. The British soldiers regrouped and marched on to Concord, another six or seven miles inland, where they destroyed the ammunition and then confronted another—larger—group of local troops. Two Americans and three British were killed, with more wounded on both sides.

Meanwhile, the people of Lexington buried their dead and tended to their wounded. Gradually, they realized that those same British troops would soon be marching back through Lexington, wearily making their way to Boston. This time the local militia, aided by many others from the surrounding area, would be ready. When the royal troops arrived, they found no soldiers standing on the green. Instead, as they plodded on, they suffered being shot at from behind stone fences, large trees, and scattered farm buildings. This was warfare? Yes, Yankee warfare, developed over decades in many earlier battles.[2]

The British retreat became a rout, as militiamen, aided by boys too young to serve officially, fired from cover, reloaded, aimed, and fired again. Only with the coming of darkness did the British manage to make their way back to the protection of His Majesty's warships. British casualties numbered nearly 300, those of the Yankees fewer than 100. But the die had been cast. King George III announced that "the New England governments are in a state of rebellion." But he was wrong: all 13 colonies prepared to join the fight.

The Second Continental Congress, scheduled to convene five days after Franklin's arrival back home, unanimously chose the recently returned agent as a delegate from his own colony. This

Congress—eager to show that the rebellion was not limited to a few New England radicals—in June appointed a Virginian, George Washington, to head a Continental Army that did not yet exist. But if this was a measure of American commitment and resolve, the British provided their own measure as they dispatched their most experienced generals to assist General Gage in putting a stop to this impromptu and possibly short-lived rebellion.[3]

In the Congress, Benjamin Franklin accepted every duty thrust upon him. After all, he had more experience, more intimate knowledge of British intentions and wiles, more accumulated wisdom than most of the other delegates. He served on the committee for foreign affairs, the committee to deal with monetary matters, and the committee on safety. Franklin, at 70 the oldest man at the convention, was also one of the busiest. "In the morning at six I am at the Committee of Safety," he wrote to Joseph Priestley back in England. That group meets until about 9 o'clock, "when I am at the Congress, and that sits till after four in the afternoon." Franklin was impressed with the delegates' diligence, their unanimity, and their faithful attendance.[4]

Franklin did everything but make speeches; the Continental Congress had all the orators that it needed, and Franklin concluded that his best talents lay elsewhere. In July he accepted appointment as postmaster general, a post with which he had some experience under English jurisdiction. Now, with a freer hand, he reorganized the whole system, with the help of his son-in-law, Richard Bache. The Congress paid Franklin a salary of $1,000 per year, which he donated for the care of wounded soldiers. The royal post office slowly faded away, and the post office that Franklin introduced, now operating wholly under American control, has survived in its essentials to the present time.[5]

In August 1775, King George III declared all the colonies, not just Massachusetts, to be in rebellion. And in October, as head of a committee of three, Franklin met with General George Washington in Massachusetts to inspect what army there was and to confer with the general about his most pressing needs. Washington received the support of Franklin and the others to impose severe discipline on troops largely innocent of military regimen. And he won agreement on such mundane but essential details as how much meat, bread, milk, beer, and cider should be allotted to each soldier. Finally, Franklin wrote to the Continental Congress: "The General then requested that the Committee would represent to the Congress the necessity of having money constantly and regularly sent." Washington's requests for money would in the years ahead only grow more pressing, even frantic.[6]

Franklin calculated the cost of the war, but he was not depressed by the outcome of his calculations. If he could count the number of candles that daylight saving time would save, so he could reckon the amount of sacrifice that each family must make in order to support an army. To maintain an army of some 20,000 soldiers, which the committee recommended, the country needed to raise about £100,000 per month. "If 500,000 families will each spend a shilling a week less, or earn a shilling a week more," he wrote to Richard Bache on October 19, 1775, "they may pay the whole sum without otherwise feeling it." But such neat calculations failed to account for the stubborn realities that made raising money a persisting, haunting problem for the Americans.[7]

In December 1775 Franklin wrote essays and songs on behalf of the growing rebellion, even as he contributed a war cry that Thomas Jefferson adopted as his own: "Rebellion to tyrants is obedience to God." He inclined more and more in the direction of complete separation, but sadly his son, William, royal governor of New Jersey, moved in the opposite direction. Early in 1776, colonial authorities placed William under house arrest, his loyalty to the American cause now being openly questioned. And in June, he was arrested and removed to Connecticut, where he was placed in prison.[8]

William's father neither visited him nor came to his aid. Many years later, Franklin wrote this to William: "Indeed, nothing has ever hurt me so much and affected me with such keen Sensations, as to find myself deserted in my old Age by my only Son, and not only deserted but taking up Arms against me, in a Cause wherein my good Fame, Fortune and Life were all at Stake." On his own behalf, William pleaded that, as a royal governor, he had a duty to his king. Perhaps, Franklin replied, but there was a higher duty than that: of a son to his father.[9]

While Benjamin Franklin was still in London, he was asked to intercede on behalf of a young man, down on his luck, who was most interested in immigrating to America. Franklin quickly wrote a letter to his son-in-law, Richard Bache, recommending "this ingenious, worthy young man" by the name of Thomas Paine. Franklin had no great expectations about Paine's future, but simply wanted to help him survive. "If you can put him in a way of obtaining employment as a clerk, or assistant tutor in a school," Franklin wrote, "so that he may procure a subsistence at least . . . you will do well and much oblige your affectionate father." Paine made the voyage, arriving in October 1774, and found employment as a tutor and a printer's assistant, but most of all soon discovered his true vocation as propagandist and pamphleteer.[10]

In January 1776 he produced the most widely read tract of the American Revolution, *Common Sense.* Paine argued vigorously—and persuasively—that the time for discussion and deliberation was past. Now action must be taken. "We have it in our power,"

Paine wrote, "to begin the world over again." Monarchy's time had passed, he argued; now "a New Order of the Ages" would introduce republicanism: "a government of our own is our natural right." Paine's 47-page tract quickly sold out, only to be reprinted time and again, devoured by a public growing impatient for decisive action.[11]

In March 1776 the Continental Congress appointed Franklin as a member of a three-man commission to Canada to see if greater investment of monies and men should be expended in an effort to capture Quebec. They found that American supply lines were stretched too thin, while the winter blizzards had taken their toll on lives and morale. Moreover, all indications suggested British reinforcements were already on their way. To the disappointment of the American commanders in Canada, the commissioners had no news of additional supplies and no funds; they were there merely to observe and make recommendations.

The Congress received this report from Franklin (along with Samuel Chase and Charles Carroll): "If money cannot be had to support your army here with honour, so as to be respected instead of hated by the people, we repeat it as our firm and unanimous opinion that it is better immediately to withdraw." This position came hard for Franklin, who long held that Canada should be neither French nor British, but American—a 14th colony, if you will. But the political and military winds blew in other directions.[12]

Back with the Second Continental Congress in Philadelphia after the difficult and dangerous Canadian mission, Franklin found the sentiment for independence rapidly rising. The delegates, too, had read *Common Sense*. Virginia took the lead by proposing in early June that the Congress now "declare the United Colonies free and independent states, absolved from all allegiance to, or dependence upon, the Crown or Parliament of Great Britain." A straw vote—that is, an unofficial vote—was taken to determine the sentiments of the colonies, with the result that only seven colonies voted in favor of Virginia's resolution. Those opposed did not necessarily disagree with the declaration; they questioned only the timing.

It was agreed to put off the final vote for three weeks, but not to waste any time in the interim. The Congress appointed a committee of five to prepare some suitable statement of principle on which, it was fervently hoped, all colonies could agree. The committee consisted of two men from New England, John Adams and Roger Sherman; two from the middle colonies, Franklin and Robert Livingston; and only one from the south, Thomas Jefferson, but he would be named chairman. The immediate task was to prepare a draft that would convey the colonial position without ambiguity. Jefferson might have preferred to yield this assignment to his seniors, either Franklin or Adams, but both urged the younger man—who had already acquired a reputation for style—to proceed with a first draft. Other members, meanwhile, would lobby those delegates still hesitating or waiting for further instructions from home. The problem, an impatient John Adams stated, was to get 13 clocks to strike at exactly the same time.[13]

On July 2, 1776, the Congress took a vote on the declaration for the record, with the happy result that unanimity was at last achieved. The Congress then turned to Jefferson's draft, which was debated and amended on July 2, July 3, and July 4. Jefferson found this revision process exceedingly painful, though Franklin tried with humor to ease some of the discomfort. But finally, the Congress had not only a vote for independence but also a declaration stating the grounds upon which that vote was taken. For all the hesitation and verbal wrangling exhibited in the Continental Congress, once the Declaration of Independence was printed and circulated throughout the colonies, wild celebrations erupted. Fireworks exploded, bells rang, crowds cheered, and prayers for the Congress now replaced those routinely offered for the Crown. But as Franklin and the other delegates well knew, a long and difficult road lay ahead.[14]

On July 16, friends and fellow citizens elected Franklin president of the Pennsylvania convention to revise its own state constitution, an honor that Franklin deeply appreciated, even though he would still spend most of his time with the Congress. Though Franklin never wavered in his support of the war effort, he nevertheless wished "most earnestly for peace." The Congress took advantage of that sincere wish by persuading him to make one last gesture in the direction of conciliation. British admiral Richard Howe, posted on Staten Island, was a military leader with whom Franklin had long enjoyed a warm relationship, and who now revealed a willingness to receive Franklin and others as official representatives of the Continental Congress.

In an exchange of letters, Franklin indicated that little could be expected of yet another conference because of Great Britain's "abounding pride and deficient wisdom." Nevertheless, in September 1776 Franklin—with John Adams of Massachusetts and Edward Rutledge of South Carolina—met with Howe, who stated that His Majesty was at last ready to accede to the demands that Franklin and others had repeatedly made in 1774–75. Now, however, they had a new demand: full and free independence of the several colonies, now states. And that, neither Howe nor the king was prepared to grant.[15]

So the War for Independence continued. It would probably be a long war, and with no navy and a wholly volunteer army, America needed help. Foreign aid from some source was absolutely essential. France, at war with England four times in less than a century, appeared the most likely prospect for such aid. And once more Benjamin Franklin appeared the most likely person for the Congress to call upon to plead the American cause.

In September the Congress elected him, along with Silas Deane, the Connecticut lawyer and diplomat, and Arthur Lee of Virginia, as commissioners to France. On October 27 Franklin boarded an oceangoing vessel one more time, accompanied by two grandsons. Temple, now 17, would serve as his secretary. Seven-year-old Benjamin Franklin Bache, son of Sarah and Richard, would benefit from private schooling abroad and avoid the imminent dangers of a revolution certain to erupt in and around Philadelphia. Now Franklin moved to another career, another role, another array of challenges for the elder statesman.[16]

Franklin and his grandsons arrived in France on December 3, and the threesome made their way slowly to Paris in the next three weeks. Secretly, Franklin met with France's foreign minister, the Comte de Vergennes, with whom he would have to deal over the next nine years in an effort to secure France's aid, perhaps even its alliance. France at this point was officially neutral. So far as the American war was concerned, the French considered it a civil war between Britain and its colonies. Some private companies might be organized to render aid in the form of arms and supplies, but none of this involved France in any official capacity.

If Vergennes's position was difficult, so was Franklin's. The Congress had appointed the three commissioners to France, but the trio failed to agree among themselves on either the process or the substance of negotiations with France. The Congress, more-over, did not speak in a unified voice, as varying factions jockeyed for influence and control. Too, the maddening slowness of communication led to either frustration or unauthorized action: three months or more to send a question from Paris to Philadelphia and to get a reply back to the commissioners. And if the reply failed to clarify, as was often the case, or the situation had radically altered, as also was often the case, then the tedious process had to begin all over again.

In January 1777, King Louis XVI formally received the commissioners' request for the badly needed financial assistance. The king responded with a grant of 2 million livres, roughly something over $300,000. This welcome gift was not so much an embrace of American republicanism—after all, Louis had a vested interest in the preservation of monarchy—as it was an effort to check Britain's pretensions as a world power. Perhaps the North American continent, where France had been humiliated in the French and Indian War, presented the best opportunity for France to avenge itself against its old and continuing enemy. But could France do more?[17]

The answer to that question depended in part on the military fortunes of General Washington's forces in the field. And in that respect, things were not going well for the Americans. After the battles at Lexington and Concord, British forces won a battle, though at a great cost, at Boston's Bunker Hill. Boston was spared a long siege when British general William Howe decided to abandon that port for the one in New York City, where a major British buildup took place. At great risk, Washington challenged the British in New York. Only his skill in retreat saved most of his army. Washington had the opportunity to become even better at retreats—across the Hudson into New Jersey, across the Delaware into Pennsylvania. The British Navy, meanwhile, roamed up and down the Atlantic coast at will, for Washington had no ships with which to challenge it.

In October 1777, the Americans at last won a major victory, at Saratoga in upstate New York. The British general John ("Gentleman Johnny") Burgoyne surrendered nearly 6,000 troops, with all their supporting arms, artillery, and military supplies. However cheering this victory proved to be to Washington and his generals, when the news reached France in December it provided even more cheer, for now France was prepared to enter into an open alliance with the United States. France's decision was spurred by its fear that Britain might quickly make peace and shut off all possibilities of a profitable American trade with France. Such an alliance also gave France the excuse for rebuilding its own navy.

Quickly, France officially recognized the United States as a separate power, giving Britain no choice but to declare war on France, which it did in June 1778. Before that, however, Franklin had succeeded in February in signing treaties of amity, commerce, and military alliance with France. The terms of these agreements bound both sides to make no separate peace with England, and France agreed to take no territory in North America. Another French grant to America, this time of about $2 million, further cemented the relationship between the two countries.[18]

Soon after the treaty signing, Franklin moved out of Paris into an attractive suburb, Passy, on the road toward Versailles. Here, on an inviting estate with spacious gardens, Franklin spent the remainder of his time in France. Living comfortably, with many servants, a cellar stocked with fine wines, and amiable neighbors nearby, Franklin could almost forget his torments from gout, bladder or kidney stones, and other infirmities of old age. The public adulation that he received in the fashionable circles of society also helped him to ignore his physical infirmities.

Franklin was already a well-known figure in France long before his arrival late in 1776. His scientific experiments, especially with electricity, gave him immediate entrée into intellectual circles, as did his many writings. As the object of popular acclaim, Franklin played the part to the hilt. He even dressed for the part—not in the fine velvets and silver buckles that he wore in England, but in the plain, simple style of a common American. When his daughter, Sally, wrote to ask that her father send her some fine French linen and other luxuries, he replied on June 3, 1779, that "you sending for long black pins, and lace, and *feathers!* disgusted me as much as if you had put salt into my strawberries." He always preached frugality (though not necessarily practiced at Passy), he wrote, and "I cannot in conscience or decency encourage the contrary . . . in furnishing my children with foolish modes and luxuries." And as for feathers, "my dear girl, [these] may be had in America from every cock's tail."[19]

So Franklin—and those dear to him—served as a symbol of democracy, the epitome of a new and classless society. His beaver hat immediately set a new style in Paris, and he drew crowds wherever he went. When he attended sessions of the French Parliament, admirers applauded as he arrived or left. Leading artists painted him or sculpted his likeness. His portrait appeared on medallions and snuffboxes, even in rings. In some amazement, he wrote to Sally, "your father's face [is] as well known as that of the moon." And France's Baron Turgot coined the epigram for Franklin that stuck: "He snatched fire from the heavens and the sceptre from the tyrant's hands."[20]

Franklin entertained—and was entertained by—the ladies of Paris during his years there. His letters to particular women were flirtatious, amusing, and filled with memories of the many happy evenings spent in their company. *Réunion des Musées Nationaux / Art Resource, N.Y.*

As in England, he made friends with intellectual leaders and was accepted in their circle without reservation. His close relationship with France's most visible philosopher and fellow satirist, Voltaire, is representative of this warmth. At a 1778 meeting of the Royal Academy of Sciences, Franklin and Voltaire, properly introduced, bowed respectfully to each other, but the audience wanted more. Here, these two representatives of a new age, one from the Old World and one from the New, must be more demonstrative. Finally, the two men understood what those present wanted: a full embrace, with kisses on the cheeks, a symbolic uniting of their common intellectual adventure. In that same year, Franklin assisted in Voltaire's initiation into the Parisian Masonic

lodge. And when Voltaire died soon after, Benjamin Franklin offi-
ciated at the funeral of France's great man, who was deeply suspicious of all priests.[21]

Franklin's acceptance in high society was not limited to the
philosophers, historians, or other major figures of the Enlighten-
ment, that intellectual awakening of the 18th century. The ladies
loved him, and he returned their sentiments. Two of his favorites
were Madame Brillon, a neighbor in Passy, and Madame Helvétius,
who entertained Franklin regularly at her salon, a sparkling assembly of Paris's cultural and artistic leaders. Madame Brillon, a
devout Catholic and a married woman half Franklin's age, engaged
in flirtatious banter with Franklin both in person and in many
letters. Franklin gave as good as he got, confessing that the com-
mandment not to covet his neighbor's wife was one that he broke
all too often.[22]

Madame Helvétius, a widow, entertained on a lavish scale, including in her salon not only Baron Turgot, author of the Franklin
epigram, and novelist-philosopher Denis Diderot, but also David
Hume of Scotland. Franklin relished the conversation, but no less
the endless flirtation. Grateful that she had given him so many of
her days, Franklin thought it only fitting that he offer her some of
his nights. That offer, so far as the historical record reveals, was
never accepted.

Affairs of state, however, did intrude. Arthur Lee, Franklin's
co-commissioner, was a constant irritant to Franklin, and his constant critic. Lee alienated nearly everyone in France, destroying
any possible usefulness he might have had as a commissioner. He
suspected Franklin of misuse of funds. The accusation, however,
was weakened by the fact that he suspected almost everyone else
of the same. Silas Deane found himself charged with misappro-

priation of funds, and when he was called before the Congress in Philadelphia, he had difficulty explaining all his expenses. The Congress determined to replace him, sending in his stead John Adams, who was accompanied by his remarkable wife, Abigail.[23]

Adams, of course, had established a reputation in Massachusetts and in the Continental Congress as a leading revolutionary, a political theorist of no small merit, and a man of action. But although Adams respected Franklin's wide and deserved acclaim, these two powerful figures did not get along. When asked once about his relationship with Adams, Franklin replied that it was one of civility but not of intimacy.

Adams's comments were more extended. As he noted in his diary: "The Life of Dr. Franklin was a Scene of continual dissipation. I could never obtain the favor of his Company in a Morning before Breakfast which would have been the most convenient time to read over the Letters and papers, deliberate on their contents, and decide upon the Substance of the Answers." No sooner was a leisurely breakfast concluded, Adams continued, than a crowd of carriages brought "all Sorts of People" to "have the honour to see the great Franklin." When, finally, all the visitors left, "it was time to dress to go to Dinner," which, in Franklin's case, usually meant going out. He almost never declined an invitation, Adams concluded, especially to an elegant home and a sumptuous dinner.[24]

This characterization was not fair, as Franklin kept up a steady correspondence. He even bought a small printing press that enabled him to speed up many of the routine requests—including, as the official representative of the United States, the printing of passports—that came to him. But Franklin was feeling his age, and in March 1781 even submitted his resignation to the Congress. "I have passed my seventy-fifth year," he wrote, "and I find that the long and severe fit of gout which I had last winter has shaken me considerably, and I am yet far from having recovered the bodily strength I before enjoyed." He did not look with favor on any more long sea voyages, and even considered taking his retirement in France. The Continental Congress declined to accept his resignation; instead, the members appointed Franklin, along with four others, to a Peace Commission in the early summer of 1781.[25]

Peace with Britain had been discussed with varying degrees of seriousness for some time, with Spain offering to serve as intermediary between Britain and France. But after the surrender of British general Cornwallis at Yorktown, Virginia, in October 1781, peace seemed a real possibility. Franklin would represent the middle states, along with a New Yorker, John Jay, who was currently in Spain working with that ally. (Spain, however, unlike the French, contributed little money to the American cause.) John Adams, currently in Holland seeking a loan from the Dutch, would represent New England. And two men were chosen to speak for the South: Thomas Jefferson of Virginia and Henry Laurens of South Carolina. But Jefferson declined to serve, and Laurens was captured at sea by the British. So in effect, only three men served as peace commissioners: Franklin, Jay, and Adams. And they were instructed to keep France fully informed of any and all discussions with the British.

Franklin had no objection to keeping France informed, but Adams did. He and the French foreign minister, Vergennes, had virtually stopped speaking to each other before Adams left for Holland. Adams, moreover, saw Franklin as little more than a tool in the hands of the French. Jay, recently arrived from rough treatment and many indignities in Spain, trusted neither the Spanish nor the French. And so the three commissioners began quietly and secretly to talk directly with the British, who were weary of the long war and seemed ready to bring it to an end.[26]

During the fall of 1782, these unofficial conversations continued, until by the end of November essential agreement had been reached on all the major points. At this juncture, Franklin apologetically informed Vergennes of what had been going on. Vergennes protested, but softly. He too was weary of the war, and of the constant drain on the state treasury. So now all the unofficial language could become official, and on September 3, 1783, the Treaty of Paris was signed.

From the American point of view, the terms were remarkably generous. Britain acknowledged the sovereign independence of each state, named one by one. This point was non-negotiable. The territory of the United States would stretch all the way to the Mississippi, with full navigation rights from the great river's source in the north to the Gulf of Mexico included. That was more territory than most Americans expected and more than France wanted Britain to grant—though Franklin (that "old conjuror," as Adams called him) calmly asked for all of Canada as well. Adams successfully fought for fishing rights off the coast of Newfoundland—the "gold mines" of New England, as he named them. Prisoners of war on both sides would be released, and Britain agreed to withdraw all armies and garrisons from North America. Remarkably generous indeed.

Britain, for its part, gained very little in the formal treaty, aside from an end to the fighting. It won the right to collect debts due to its merchants, and loyalists who lost all their properties and estates would have the right to seek redress from the individual states, but with no guarantees specified. Franklin had said that there was never a good war or a bad peace. This peace, at any rate, was far from bad.[27]

With the arrival of peace, Franklin could turn his attention to many other matters. In 1784 he worked on treaties with other European nations, and received yet more money from France—a total of about $21 million over the war years and immediately after. Because of the high regard in which he was held, the Vatican sought his advice in selecting an ecclesiastical head of the Roman Catholic Church in America. He recommended John Carroll of Maryland, and that advice was followed.[28]

Franklin in 1784 also accepted appointment to a French royal commission to investigate the claims of the believers in "animal magnetism" (or Mesmerism, akin to hypnotism) to cure all manner of aches and ills. Franklin's official report dismissed the claims as unfounded, though he had little optimism that the fad would quickly pass away. "There is a wonderful deal of credulity in the world," he noted in his report, "and deceptions as absurd have supported themselves for ages." He even took time to question whether the warlike eagle was the best bird to serve as a national symbol of America—perhaps, he suggested, the native turkey would be better. Finally, in this busy year, he requested from the Continental Congress permission to return home.[29]

It took the Congress nearly a year to say yes and to appoint Thomas Jefferson to succeed him as minister to France. Sometime after Jefferson arrived, Franklin left for home in June 1785. He sailed for England, visited briefly with his son, William, in July, when they reached a measure of reconciliation, and then set out for Philadelphia once more. On September 14, he docked at the Market Street wharf, his arrival announced to all the city by the booming of cannon. Bells rang as he made his way a few blocks to his house, which the British had occupied and ransacked. There he greeted grandchildren ("four new Prattlers, who cling around the knees of their Grand Papa, and afford me great pleasure") whom he now saw for the first time. "The affectionate Welcome I met with from my fellow-Citizens," he wrote to John Jay and his wife, "is far beyond my Expectation."[30]

B. Franklin on J. Adams

In 1782 New York's powerful delegate to the Second Conti-nental Congress, Robert R. Livingston, complained to Franklin in Paris that he had not had replies from Franklin to his recent letters. Franklin responded on July 22, 1783, with an apology, but also with an indication of major divisions among the peace commissioners, specifi-cally between John Adams and himself.

I ought not, however, to conceal from you, that one of my Colleagues [Adams] is of a very different Opinion from me in these Matters. He thinks the French Minister one of greatest Enemies of our Country, that he would have [restricted] our Boundaries, to prevent the Growth of our people; contracted our Fishery, to obstruct the Increase of our Seaman; and retained the Royalists among us, to keep us divided; that he privately opposes all our Negociations with foreign Courts, and afforded us, dur-ing the War, the Assistance we receiv'd only to keep it alive, that we might be so much the more weaken'd by it; that to think of Gratitude to France is the greatest of Fol-lies, and that to be influenc'd by it would ruin us. He makes no Secret of his having these Opinions, expresses them publicly, sometime in presence of the English Min-isters, and speaks of hundreds of Instances which he could produce in Proof of them. None of which, how-ever, have yet appear'd to me. . . .

I write this to put you on your guard, (believing it my duty, tho' I know that I hazard by it a mortal Enemy), and to caution you respecting the Insinuations of this Gentle-man against this Court, and the Instances he supposes of their ill will to us, which I take to be as imaginary as I know his Fancies to be, that the Coumt de V[ergennes] and myself are continually plotting against him, and em-ploying the News-Writers of Europe to deprecate his Character, &c. . . . I am persuaded, however, that he means well for his Country, is always an honest Man, often a wise one, but sometimes, and in some things, absolutely out of his senses.

Seven

NEW NATION AND AGED PATRIARCH

What is serving God? 'Tis doing Good to man.
—Poor Richard's Almanack, 1747

IN THE LATTER YEARS OF THE 18TH CENTURY, AMERICA ATTRACTED many Europeans to its shores. The promise of both land and liberty proved irresistible to those frozen out of land ownership and to those trapped in a class-bound society. If a young nation could take on the British Empire and prevail militarily against it, then what did the future hold for that country and its citizens? From afar, no limitations or obstacles seemed to threaten that future.

Franklin found himself besieged by French citizens who wished to share in that future. After offering advice on an individual basis, he decided by 1784 to publish a brief guide, *Information to Those Who Would Remove to America.* Not only did he offer here helpful advice, but he hinted at his own view of the essence of the American experiment. Yes, he asserted, America was a land of opportunity, but only for those prepared to work. Because population was steadily increasing, the chances for making a living were good. Farmers willing to till the soil were welcome; artisans with any degree of talent could soon open their own businesses. "People do not enquire concerning a Stranger, *What is he?*" said Franklin, but "*What can he do?*" Moreover, "if he has any useful Art, he is welcome; and if he exercises it and behaves well, he will be respected by all who know him."[1]

On the other hand, if one was of noble birth in Europe and was so deluded to think that this distinction alone would sustain him in America, Franklin cautioned, he would be greatly disappointed. "In Europe it has indeed its Value, but it is a Commodity that cannot be carried to a worse Market than to that of America." There were no lords and ladies in America, and no rigid class structure to keep nine-tenths of the population in submissive poverty. Very few in America would be called rich, but very few were as miserable as the poor in Europe. In his country, Franklin added, "it is rather a general happy Mediocrity that prevails."[2]

All must work in America—even the farm animals. In his guide, Franklin related an anecdote, which he attributed to an African American, explaining that on the farm only the hog did not work. He ate and drank when he pleased, slept when he pleased, and indeed lived "like a Gentleman." So if one aspired in America to live "idly on the Labour of others," doing nothing of value himself, he would be classified with the hogs, for they were America's only "gentlemen." Much better, he advised, for prospective emigrants to America to prove that they were descended from carpenters, weavers, tanners, or farmers than that they were of "noble" blood. In short, Franklin concluded, America might indeed be a land of opportunity, but only to those who recognized that it was first and foremost "the Land of Labour."[3]

When Franklin arrived in Philadelphia in the fall of 1785, he was given a short rest before being asked again to assume public duties. The new nation was threatening to fall apart as the weakness and lawlessness of the recently formed government unnerved many Americans. Under the Articles of Confederation, adopted by most states by 1779, some authority was given to the Congress, but most authority remained with the states—states jealous of their sovereignty and suspicious of any effort by the central government to diminish it. That central government, essentially run by committees and from no fixed capital city, found itself in the position of having to beg the states for money, men, or authority to regulate commerce—or much of anything else. Then an uprising of farmers in western Massachusetts in late 1786, known as Shays's Rebellion, shook complacency further, so that sentiment grew for a more effective government: one that could command respect both at home and abroad.

Under this pressure, the Confederation Congress agreed to call a convention to meet in Philadelphia in May 1787. Each state legislature would name delegates to this assembly, and Pennsylvania promptly named the 81-year-old Benjamin Franklin as one its eight representatives. Franklin agreed to serve in what came to be known as the Constitutional Convention. His very presence lent a needed legitimacy to a gathering that soon went far beyond what most had anticipated as its limited duty: namely, to revise the Articles of Confederation. Franklin played no active part in most of the debates and discussions regarding a new constitution, leaving that role to a 36-year-old from Virginia, James Madison. George Washington, finally persuaded to leave the many tasks awaiting him at his Mount Vernon estate, presided over the convention, and these two widely respected Americans, Washington and Franklin, helped ensure the necessary broad acceptance of the results of a summer's secret deliberations.[4]

Franklin had earlier proposed that under the Articles of Confederation voting be proportional to the population of each state. Naturally, the smaller states objected, fearing that they would be pushed aside by the likes of such large states as Pennsylvania and Virginia. The result was that each state had a single vote, and that on major matters unanimity of all 13 was required. Now, the 1787 Convention faced the familiar dilemma: how to distribute power in a way that respected both the sovereignty of each state and the varying strengths of the population among the states. Franklin proposed and pushed for what came to be called the Great Compromise: in the Senate, each state (large or small) would have equal representation, while in the House, the number of representatives would be based on the population of each state.[5]

Franklin designed this and other Continental currency; he intended the complex patterns to discourage counterfeiters. Convinced of the necessity of a paper currency, Franklin lobbied hard with the Pennsylvania Assembly for its use; as a consequence, he was assigned to print the currency—"a very profitable Jobb," he reported. *Philadelphia Museum of Art, Gift of Mr. and Mrs. John D. Rockefeller Jr., 1946*

A major hurdle had been cleared, though of course many more compromises and adjustments had to be made. And not everyone was pleased with the results. Of the 55 delegates who attended the convention over the course of the summer, only 39 signed the final document presented on September 17, 1787. Would that be enough to ensure ratification by the people in their own separate state conventions? Franklin thought so. During those many long weeks of deliberations, Franklin looked at the artist's portrayal of a sun, low in the horizon, on the back of Washington's chair. Franklin had often asked himself, according to the *Records of the Convention,* whether that sun was rising or setting. "But now at length," he commented to James Madison as he signed the Constitution, "I have the happiness to know that it is a rising and not a setting Sun."[6]

Franklin did not make speeches at this stage in his life, but in the closing days of the convention he did write out one for fellow delegate James Wilson to read for him, as Franklin's voice was not as strong as it had once been. His remarks had as their clear purpose winning approval for the newly drafted Constitution. He thought perfection too lofty and unrealistic a goal to expect from an assembly of men with local interests, contrary passions, and personal prejudices. One could only marvel, he believed, that they came as close to perfection as they did. "Thus I consent, Sir, to this Constitution," Wilson declared on Franklin's behalf, "because I expect no better, and because I am not sure that it is not the best."[7]

It was the flaw of mankind, especially in religion, Franklin noted, to consider its own judgments as free from all possible error. But on this critical occasion, Franklin urged that every member of the convention might "doubt a little of his own Infallibility." So the Constitution was signed, then sent out to the people for ratification, state by state, in the months that followed. By the summer of 1788 a sufficient number of states (the Constitution required a minimum of nine) had ratified it so that a congress could be organized, elections set, and George Washington chosen as the first president. The new nation had been reborn.[8]

Franklin's last public service was rendered on behalf of the abolition of slavery. In late 1787 he accepted the presidency of the newly reorganized Pennsylvania Society for Promoting the Abolition of Slavery. Then the familiar pattern of earlier efforts repeated itself: raising funds, gathering broad support, petitioning Congress (which said this was a matter for the states), and anticipating objections to their aims. "Slavery is such an atrocious debasement of human nature," Franklin wrote on behalf of the society (in "Address to the Public"), "that its very extirpation, if not performed with solicitous care, may sometimes open a source of serious evils." That is, slaves must be emancipated with great caution so that they would not become a burden to society or a mockery to their own new freedom.[9]

More needed to be done by way of preparation, training, and education, Franklin explained, to make certain that the ex-slave was ready to seize the advantages of his new status. The newly emancipated must be instructed and advised, Franklin asserted, and must cultivate "the habits of industry" in order to find employment "suited to their age, sex, talents, and other circumstances." Plans must also be formulated for the education of the children "calculated for their future situation in life." All this would require monetary support, Franklin explained, far beyond "the present ordinary funds of the Society." Therefore, the Society "will gratefully receive any donations or subscriptions for this purpose."[10]

Franklin refused to let the subject go without resorting once more to satire. He took the speech of a Georgia delegate to Congress in support of slavery and put the same sentiments in the mouth of an African Muslim justifying the keeping of Christians as slaves. "Let us hear no more of this detestable Proposition, the Manumission of Christian slaves," the Muslim ruler concluded. For to take that radical step would "create universal Discontent, and provoke Insurrections, to the endangering of Government and producing general Confusion." Franklin, who came to his abolitionist position late in life, still anticipated by a generation or so the more open and widespread agitation for the emancipation of the slaves.[11]

Franklin did not solve the problem of slavery, nor did any other single man. Only a long and tragic war could do that. Nor did he solve the problem of the Indian being steadily pushed westward by the white man's unquenchable thirst for land, and ever more land. But, like William Penn before him, Franklin tried to deal honestly with the several tribes he encountered, to respect their cultures, and make every effort to see their point of view.

Why were the Indians called "savages"? he inquired. "It is only because their manners differ from ours, which we think the Perfection of Civility." In his "Remarks" written in France in 1783, he noted that the Indians listened respectfully to the missionaries' biblical stories, but then these worthy gentlemen gave no respect to the Indians' stories. The English, said the Indians, gave Indian children an education, *their* education, then sent them back to us "ignorant of every means of living in the Woods." These "educated" children could not build a cabin, or hunt a deer, or take an enemy: "they were totally good for nothing." From the Indian point of view, Franklin explained, it made equal sense "if the Gentlemen of Virginia will send us a dozen of their Sons." The Indians would "take Care of their Education, instruct them in all we know, and make Men of them." Whether this is Franklin's satire or that of the Indians, the point is made: differing cultures deserve the same respect.[12]

In the last year of Franklin's life, many persons still pushed and probed to learn as much about this public and private figure as possible. What made him tick? What, deep down, did he really believe about God, the Bible, Jesus? Ezra Stiles, president of Yale College and Congregational clergyman, wrote to his friend (they had often corresponded before) to inquire about his religious views. This was not just idle or "improper" curiosity, Stiles assured him, but a sincere desire to know more about his faith. Franklin responded by saying that this was the first time he had ever been asked that question. Though this may have been technically true, Franklin had frequently corresponded with friends about his opinions on religion. He had offered a revised version of the Lord's Prayer, had penned an "improved" *Book of Common Prayer,* had in 1728 written *Articles of Belief & Acts of Religion* ("a little Liturgy or Forms of Prayer for my own private Use," as he stated in his *Autobiography*), and had even provided an extra chapter for the Book of Genesis to make a case for religious toleration.[13]

But if President Stiles wanted a quick summary of his religion, he would willingly provide it.

> Here is my Creed. I believe in one God, Creator of the Universe. That he governs it by his Providence. That he ought to be worshipped. That the most acceptable Service we render to him is doing good to his other Children. That the soul of man is immortal, and will be treated with Justice in another Life respecting

its Conduct in this. These I take to be the fundamental Principles of all sound Religion, and I regard them as you do in whatever Sect I meet with them.[14]

That might work as a broad statement about religion, but was it Christianity?

Stiles wanted to know in particular what Franklin believed about Jesus of Nazareth. Franklin responded that he (like Jefferson) regarded the "System of Morals" provided by Jesus to be "the best the World ever saw or is likely to see." But on the critical question of the divinity of Jesus, Franklin acknowledged that he, along with many others who believed in a natural or rational—as opposed to a revealed—religion, did have some doubts. But this, he noted, was a question "I do not dogmatize upon, having never studied it." Then he added, with characteristic wit—writing at age 84 and near death—that he would not undertake to study the issue now, "when I expect soon an Opportunity of knowing the Truth with less Trouble."[15]

In the realm of religion, Franklin did not dogmatize about very much. He was respectful of the religious views of others, contributed to most religious groups in Philadelphia when they were building new churches, and maintained warm personal relationships with most of the clergy. But Franklin gave up going to church after he tired of sermons that gave their attention mainly (as he saw it) to the husks of religion rather than the kernel. And that kernel, he believed, was doing good to others.

At the Day of Judgment, Franklin wrote, we will not be asked what we believe, but what we have done. And to another correspondent he wrote, many years earlier in 1753, that he had a good opinion of religion in general—he only wished "it were more productive of Good Works." He added: "I mean real good Works,

Works of Kindness, Charity, Mercy, and Publick Spirit." All this, as opposed to "Holiday-keeping, Sermon-Reading or Hearing, performing Church Ceremonies, or making long Prayers." On this issue of morality over dogma, Franklin was more than willing to dogmatize, as long as he had the strength to do so.[16]

But Franklin's strength rapidly waned. In the last year of his life, Franklin never left his bedroom. And on April 10 his last illness struck, with fever, difficulty in breathing, and finally a state of total lethargy. In the words of his physician, on April 17, 1790, "about eleven o'clock at night, he quietly expired, closing a long and useful life of eighty-four years and three months."[17]

Many years before his death, when he was feeling much friskier, Franklin the printer composed the following epitaph for himself:

The Body of
B. Franklin Printer
(Like the Cover of an Old Book
Its Contents torn out
And stript of its Lettering & Gilding)
Lies here, Food for Worms,
But the Work shall not be lost;
For it will (as he believ'd) appear once more,
In a new and more elegant Edition
Revised and corrected
By the Author

Shortly before his death, in a more somber time, he drew up his will, where he provided a much simpler epitaph: "Benjamin and Deborah Franklin 1790." Husband was buried next to his wife in Philadelphia's Christ Church cemetery, alongside their young son Franky.[18]

Thousands attended his funeral service on April 21, and the next day James Madison proposed that members of the House of Representatives wear mourning for a month; the motion passed unanimously. A memorial service the following year, held in Philadelphia's large German Lutheran Church, gave the whole nation the opportunity to pay its respects. President George Washington and his wife, Martha, attended, as did Vice President John Adams and his wife, Abigail. Most of the nation's senators and representatives came down from New York City (the temporary capital) for the occasion. Many others crowded into the church, including of course the fraternity of printers. The eulogy was delivered by the Reverend William Smith, an Anglican clergyman and frequent enemy of Franklin's. But the memorial service in 1791 was not a time for airing old grievances or reopening old wounds. It was a time for healing and unifying, for celebrating and honoring.

And Smith rose to the occasion honorably. Franklin, he declared, was a New World luminary, an Old Testament patriarch, a classical-world Hercules, "a splendid sun of science," and a revered citizen of the world. "Let all thy fellow citizens," Smith intoned, "consider thee as their guardian-genius, still present and presiding amongst them." And this, of course, was what a new, untried nation, poised on the edge of the unknown, needed to hear. Franklin still lived, still guided and inspired. Jefferson's tribute was equally extravagant, as he praised Franklin as "the greatest man and ornament of the age and country in which he lived." He would live on "like a star of the first magnitude in the firmament of heaven" when lesser stars will be forgotten or will have faded into darkness.[19]

If the verbal portraits were impressive, the artistic ones—especially from the French—were even more so. An etching by

This etching by French artist Marguerite Gérard is typical of how Franklin was mythologized: Franklin snatches fire (electricity) from the heavens and the sword from the hand of the tyrant (King George III). *Franklin Collection, Yale University Library, New Haven, Conn.*

Marguerite Gérard illustrated Turgot's familiar epigram, showing an omnipotent Franklin snatching fire from the heavens and the sword from the tyrant's hand. Franklin was clearly in command of all the forces of heaven and earth. Charles Le Vasseur had offered a line engraving, two years before Franklin's death, that had already made him immortal. Surrounded by the gods and goddesses of antiquity, Franklin stood for the independent American, the person who liberated America. For the French, liberty was synonymous with Franklin, and Franklin stood as their image of America.

Despite the mythologizing that these portrayals represent, Franklin remained of the earth, earthy. He tried as well to bring his contemporaries down to earth from their airy speculations. Franklin was a pragmatist. He wished to bring out the practicality, the utility of every idea. For those who avoided earthly realities, he tried to move them closer to what worked, what really made a difference. And if he could do that with a dash of humor, so much the better.

When some friends in Massachusetts named their town after him, they suggested that he might wish to donate a bell for their new steeple. They should spare themselves the expense of a steeple, he advised, and he would send them instead a gift of books, "Sense being preferable to Sound," as he explained to Richard Price, a pro-American clergyman in London. And in the endless disputes between religious institutions, Franklin supported the notion of an English friend who suggested that the chief difference between Catholics and Anglicans was that while the Roman Catholic Church was infallible, the Church of England was never wrong. In his experience, Franklin noted, people quarreled about religion as they did about food: namely, when they did not have enough of either one.[20]

In 1782 a Frenchman wrote *Letters from an American Farmer* in which he raised this question: who then is the American, this new man? In much of the 18th century, that question could be answered, whether in Philadelphia, London, or Paris, simply by pointing to the Philadelphia printer and saying, "Why, there he is!"[21]

Franklin Lobbies Against Slavery and the Slave Trade

Franklin took as his last public cause the abolition of slavery or, at the very least, the stopping of the slave trade. On the subject of buying and importing of slaves, the authors of the U.S. Constitution compromised, allowing the trade to continue another 20 years—until 1808. Franklin, unhappy with that compromise, continued to agitate for immediate action, especially in his capacity as president of the Pennsylvania Society for Promoting the Abolition of Slavery. This brief 1788 letter to John Langdon, governor of New Hampshire (and member of the Constitutional Convention), is a passionate plea for honoring the political principles set forth in the Constitution.

Sir,

The Pennsylvania Society for promoting the abolition of slavery, and the relief of free Negroes unlawfully held in bondage, have taken the liberty to ask your Excellency's acceptance of a few copies of their Constitution and the laws of the state of Pennsylvania, which relate to the objects of their Institution; also, of a copy of Thomas Clark's excellent Essay upon the Commerce and Slavery of the Africans.

The Society have heard, with great regret, that a considerable part of the slaves, who have been sold in the Southern States since the establishment of peace, have been imported in vessels fitted out in the state, over which, your Excellency presides. From your Excellency's station, they hope your influence will be exerted, hereafter, to prevent a practice which is so evidently repugnant to the political principles and form of government lately adopted by the citizens of the United States, and which cannot fail of delaying the enjoyment of the blessings of peace and liberty, by drawing down, the displeasure of the great and impartial Ruler of the Universe upon our country.

I am, in behalf of the Society,
Sir, your most obedient servant.

Notes

Prologue

1. Mark Twain, "The Late Benjamin Franklin," *Collected Tales, Sketches, Speeches, & Essays, 1852–1890* (1992), 425–27.
2. *Poor Richard Improved* (1748), in *Benjamin Franklin Writings* (1987), 1248. Hereafter *Writings*.

Chapter One

1. *Benjamin Franklin's Autobiography*, ed. J. A. Leo Lamay and P. M. Zall (1986), 6–7. Hereafter *Autobiography*.
2. Ibid., 10.
3. Ibid., 11–12.
4. Ibid., 13–14.
5. Silence Dogood #4 (May 14, 1722), *Writings*, 10–13.
6. Silence Dogood #5 (May 28, 1722), *Writings*, 14–17.
7. *Autobiography*, 9; also n. 6.
8. For a view of Franklin's extreme skepticism, from which he soon retreated, see his *Dissertation on Liberty and Necessity*, in *Writings*, 57–71.
9. Silence Dogood #8 (July 9, 1722, quoting the *London Journal*), *Writings*, 24–26.
10. *Autobiography*, 17.
11. Ibid.
Extract, pp. 13–14, from Silence Dogood #6 (June 11, 1722), *Writings*, 17–19.

Chapter Two

1. *Autobiography*, 17–19.
2. Ibid., 20–21.
3. See Rufus Jones, *Quakers in the American Colonies* (1966 [1911]).
4. *Autobiography*, 21–22.

5. Ibid., 23–25.

6. Ibid., 27–29, 33.

7. *Writings*, 57–71; *Autobiography*, 34.

8. *Autobiography*, 45, 47–48.

9. Ibid., 57.

10. Ibid., 65–71.

11. Ibid., 183 ("Biographical Notes").

12. For the fullest attention to Sally Franklin, see Claude-Anne Lopez and Eugenia W. Herbert, *The Private Franklin: The Man and His Family* (1975).

13. *Autobiography*, 64–65.

14. See J. F. Sachse, *Benjamin Franklin as a Free Mason* (1906).

15. *Autobiography*, 81–81, 87–91.

16. *Apology for Printers* (June 10, 1731), *Writings*, 171–77.

17. *Autobiography*, 79.

18. See *Writings* for generous excerpts from *Poor Richard's Almanack* and *Poor Richard Improved*, 1181–1304. For maxims quoted above, see 1281, 1200, 1212, 1208, 1186, 1277, 1201, and 1278.

19. *Autobiography*, 85, 108.

20. Ibid., 81, 82, 84, 91, 93–94, 100. Also *The Papers of Benjamin Franklin*, ed. Leonard W. Labaree et al. (1959–), 3:317. Hereafter *Papers*.

Extract, pp. 31–32, from *Autobiography*, 67–68.

CHAPTER THREE

1. *Autobiography*, 91–92; *Writings*, 295–97.

2. *Autobiography*, 97–98.

3. Ibid., 86–87.

4. Ibid.

5. Ibid., 104–5.

6. Ibid., 106–7, 103.

7. Ibid., 131.

8. Letter to Barbeu Dubourg and Thomas F. Dalibard, 1773, *The Ingenious Dr. Franklin*, ed. Nathan G. Goodman (1956 [1931]), 71–73.

9. See his immediately popular, widely translated, and often reprinted pamphlet *Experiments and Observations on Electricity Made at Philadelphia in America* (1751), in *Papers*, 4:302n.

10. *Papers* 3:372, 4:376.

11. *Writings*, 600.

12. See Walter Isaacson, *Benjamin Franklin: An American Life* (2003), 143, 172, 198, 202; H. W. Brands, *The First American: The Life and Times of Benjamin Franklin* (2000), 287, 305, 320, 393–94, 445.

13. See his letter to Sir Joseph Banks, August 30, 1783, *Writings*, 1074–8; *Autobiography* 109, 133–34; Carl Van Doren, *Benjamin Franklin* (1991 [1938]), 170.

14. *Autobiography* 39, 40.

15. Ibid., 142.

16. For the long letter to Le Roy, February 1784, see *Papers* 41:384 (unpublished).

17. Letter to Mary Stevenson, November (?) 1760, *Writings*, 779–81.

18. Ibid.

19. Letter to Giambatista Beccaria, July 13, 1762, *Writings,* 788–92.

20. "To the Authors of *The Journal of Paris*" (1784), *Ingenious Dr. Franklin*, 17–20.

21. Ibid., 22.

22. Letter to George Whately, May 23, 1785, *Writings,* 1104–10.

23. See *Ingenious Dr. Franklin*, 23–24 (gout), 74–75 (canals), 185–87 (northeast storms), and 212–14 (sunspots).

24. For the full text of these *Proposals*, see *Writings,* 323–44.

25. Ibid.

Extract, pp. 50–51, from "Of Lightning and the Method (Now Used in America) of Securing Buildings and Persons from its Mischievous Effects" (September 1767), *Writings*, 600.

CHAPTER FOUR

1. *Autobiography*, 92.

2. Ibid.

3. Ibid.

4. Ibid., 93.

5. Ibid., 93–94.

6. Letter to Peter Collinson, May 9, 1753, *Writings,* 468–74.

7. *Autobiography*, 96–97.

8. Ibid., 124, 127–28.

9. Ibid., 109–10.

10. *Pennsylvania Gazette*, May 9, 1754, *Writings,* 376–77.

11. Ibid.

12. *Autobiography*, 114.

13. Ibid., 118–20.

14. Ibid., 129–30.

15. Ibid., 135–36; also Esmond Wright, *Franklin of Philadelphia* (1986), 104–5.

16. Wright, 111.

17. Robert Middlekauf, *Benjamin Franklin and His Enemies* (1996), 113; also Wright, 106.
18. Middlekauf, 66.
19. Ibid., 70–72.
20. Isaacson, 200–5.
21. On the Stamp Act and all of its ramifications, see Edmund S. and Helen M. Morgan, *The Stamp Act Crisis: Prologue to Revolution* (1953).
22. Letter from Hall, September 6, 1765, *Papers* 12:256.
23. On his appearance before the House of Commons in 1766, see *Papers* 13:129–62.

Extract, pp. 68–69, from *Pennsylvania Gazette*, May 9, 1754.

CHAPTER FIVE
1. *Papers* 14:110–16.
2. Letter to Lord H. H. Kames, April 11, 1767, *Papers* 14:69–79.
3. "Causes of the American Discontents Before 1768," printed in *London Chronicle*, January 7, 1768, *Writings*, 607–15.
4. Ibid.
5. Ibid.
6. Wright, 182–83.
7. Ibid., 197; also *Papers* 13:233.
8. Wright, 224–26; Edmund S. Morgan, *Benjamin Franklin* (2002), 185–88.
9. Brands, 701–4.
10. Ibid.
11. Wright, 344.
12. *Writings*, 689–97.
13. Morgan, *Benjamin Franklin*, 202–3; Wright, 226–27, 228–31.
14. *Diary and Autobiography of John Adams* (1962) II, 85–86. Also see Peter D. Thomas, *Tea Party to Independence: The Third Phase of the American Revolution, 1773–1776* (1991).
15. Brands, 471–74; Isaacson, 277–79; Morgan, *Benjamin Franklin*, 202–3.
16. Letter to Joseph Galloway, February 25, 1774, *Papers* 21:508–9.
17. Letter to Charles Thomson, February 5, 1774, *Papers* 21:474.
18. H. V. Wells, *The Life and Public Service of Sam Adams* (1866), 423–24.
19. Isaacson, 288–89.
20. Ibid., 290; letter to Sarah Bache, June 3, 1779, *Writings*, 1009.

Extract, pp. 86–87, from *Writings*, 633–34.

CHAPTER SIX
1. "Extract of a Letter from Philadelphia," May 6, 1775, printed in New York on May 8 by John Anderson.

2. Joseph L. Andrews Jr., *Revolutionary Boston, Lexington, & Concord* (2002); also see Arthur B. Tourtellot, *Lexington and Concord: The Beginning of the War of the American Revolution* (1963).

3. Douglas Southall Freeman, *George Washington: A Biography*, vol. 3 (1951), chapter 18; Joseph J. Ellis, *His Excellency George Washington* (2004), 68–72.

4. Letter dated July 7, 1775, *Writings*, 904–6.

5. Wright, 238; Isaacson, 301.

6. *Papers* 22:224.

7. Letter to Richard Bache, October 19, 1775, *Papers* 22:241.

8. Isaacson, 280–83; Gordon S. Wood, *The Americanization of Benjamin Franklin* (2004), 160–63..

9. *Papers* 42:129 (unpublished).

10. Letter to Richard Bache, September 30, 1774, *Papers* 21:325.

11. Wright, 244; Brands, 509–10. For ready access to Paine's pivotal work, see *Common Sense* in the Bantam Classics series (2004).

12. Letter to John Hancock, May 8, 1776, *Papers* 22:242.

13. Brands, 510–12; Pauline Maier, *American Scripture: Making the Declaration of Independence* (1997).

14. See Benson Bobrick, *Angel in the Whirlwind: The Triumph of the American Revolution* (1997), 203–4; Maier, 156–60.

15. Wright, 254; Brands, 514–15.

16. Brands, 523–24; Wright, 254–55.

17. A. O. Aldridge, *Franklin and His French Contemporaries* (1957); Van Doren, 566–68.

18. Brands, 542–43; Van Doren, 622–23.

19. *Papers* 29:612; Wright, 263, 266–67.

20. Letter to his daughter, June 3, 1779, *Papers*, 29:612; Aldridge, 16. Turgot's epigram in Latin: *Eripuit coelo fulmen, sceptrumeque tyrannis.*

21. *The Adams Papers* (1961–), 4:80–82; Brands, 564–65.

22. For the best treatment of Franklin's social life in Paris, see Claude-Anne Lopez, *Mon Cher Papa: Franklin and the Ladies in Paris* (1990 [1966]); also Brands, 557–63.

23. Brands, 546–47, 582–83; Wright, 295, 337.

24. Wright, 268–69.

25. Brands, 598.

26. Ibid., 599–600.

27. On Franklin's eagerness to return home, see his letter to Charles Thomson, May 13, 1784, *Writings*, 1093–94.

28. Van Doren, 547, 717.

29. Ibid., 716–17; *Papers* 42:153 (unpublished); Wright, 325–26.

30. A warm letter to John Jay and his wife, September 21, 1785, *Papers* 43:434 (unpublished).

Extract, pp. 108–9, from *Writings,* 1064–65.

CHAPTER SEVEN

1. *Writings,* 975–83.

2. Ibid., 975.

3. Ibid., 976–77.

4. Wright, 340–44; Brands, 672 ff.

5. Wright, 342–43.

6. Max Farrand, *The Framing of the Constitution of the United States* (1913), 194.

7. See Wright, 343–44.

8. The election of George Washington was hardly an election at all since the prevailing assumption was that only Washington would be chosen; Adams received only enough votes to ensure that he would serve as vice president. See Ellis, 180–87.

9. *Writings,* 1154–5.

10. Ibid.

11. The title of his rich satire was "Sidi Mehemet Ibrahim on the Slave Trade," in *Writings,* 1157–60.

12. Franklin's "Remarks," written in France in 1783, may be found in *Writings,* 969–74.

13. See Edwin S. Gaustad, *Faith of the Founders* (2004 [1987]), 61–65.

14. Ibid., 65–66; *Papers* 46:400 (unpublished).

15. Gaustad, 65–66.

16. Ibid.

17. Van Doren, 778–80; Wright, 347.

18. *Writings,* 91; Isaacson, 469–70.

19. Gaustad, 68–69; Van Doren 779–81.

20. C. C. Sellers. *Benjamin Franklin in Portraiture* (1962), 284–87, 195–96, 406 (see plates 17, 32, 33, 35). On books instead of bells, see his letter to Richard Price, May 18, 1785, *Papers* 42: 721 (unpublished).

21. The question was raised by Hector St. John de Crèvecoeur in his *Letters of an American Farmer* (1782).

Extract, pp. 124–25, from *Writings,* 1169–70.

Further Reading

(Note: In addition to the sources listed below, I must express appreciation to the Packard Humanities Institute of Los Altos, California, for providing me with a CD-ROM of all Franklin's correspondence, published and unpublished. For this generosity, I am most grateful.)

The Writings of Benjamin Franklin

Autobiography. The most popular of all Franklin's works, the *Autobiography*, which covers his life up to 1757, exists in many editions. Three of the best include: *The Autobiography of Benjamin Franklin*, 2nd ed. Edited by the staff of *The Papers of Benjamin Franklin*. New Haven, Conn.: Yale University Press, 2003; J. A. Leo Lemay and P. M. Zall, eds. *Benjamin Franklin's Autobiography.* New York: W. W. Norton, 1986; Louis P. Masur. *The Autobiography of Benjamin Franklin, with Related Documents*, 2nd ed. Boston: Bedford/St. Martin's, 2003. All three have very helpful notes and carefully edited texts.

Labaree, Leonard W., et al., eds. *The Papers of Benjamin Franklin.* New Haven, Conn.: Yale University Press, 1959–. This, the definitive edition of the abundant Franklin writings, has now passed 36 volumes, with many more to come in the years ahead.

Lemay, J. A. Leo, ed. *Benjamin Franklin: Writings.* New York: Library of America, 1987. This valuable compendium, running to more than 1,600 pages, contains the major works (including many letters) from Franklin's pen. It includes excellent notes and a remarkably detailed chronology.

Biographical Works About Benjamin Franklin

Brands, H. W. *The First American: The Life and Times of Benjamin Franklin.* New York: Doubleday, 2000. A full-scale narrative biography, with many fascinating details.

Buxbaum, Melvin H. *Benjamin Franklin and the Zealous Presbyterians.* University Park: Pennsylvania State University Press, 1975. A useful account of Franklin's uneasy relationship with Philadelphia's Presbyterians.

Isaacson, Walter. *Benjamin Franklin: An American Life*. New York: Simon & Schuster, 2003. A thorough and persuasive biography, with especially helpful appendices.

Lopez, Claude-Anne. *Mon Cher Papa: Franklin and the Ladies of Paris*. Rev. ed. New Haven, Conn.: Yale University Press, 1990. The scholarship is sound, the anecdotes, personalities, and letters gripping.

Lopez, Claude-Anne, and Eugenia W. Herbert. *The Private Franklin: The Man and His Family*. New York: W. W. Norton, 1975. Franklin took his family relationships seriously, and so does this fine book.

Middlekauf, Robert. *Benjamin Franklin and His Enemies*. Berkeley: University of California Press, 1996. One can, mistakenly, glide through Franklin's amiable life without recognizing the passions of those who despised him, and his passionate contempt in return. An elegant and brilliant book.

Morgan, Edmund S. *Benjamin Franklin*. New Haven, Conn.: Yale University Press, 2002. With a deceptive simplicity and economy, Morgan presents an indelible portrait of the ever-changing Franklin. An authoritative treatment that manages not to sound authoritative.

Schiff, Stacy. *The Great Improvisation: Franklin, France, and the Birth of America*. New York: Henry Holt and Co., 2005. With impressive narrative skill, the author illuminates a vital chapter in the life of Franklin and of the new nation.

Sellers, Charles Coleman, ed. *Benjamin Franklin in Portraiture*. New Haven, Conn.: Yale University Press, 1962. An indispensable work on the artistic representations of Franklin.

Van Doren, Carl. *Benjamin Franklin*. 1938. Reprint: New York: Penguin, 1991. This exhaustive study continues to prove its value and utility.

Wood, Gordon S. *The Americanization of Benjamin Franklin*. New York: Penguin Press, 2004. A master historian separates the man from the myth and helps us to see how one was transformed into the other.

Wright, Esmond. *Franklin of Philadelphia*. Cambridge, Mass.: Harvard University Press, 1986. For readability and reliability, this biography sets a very high standard indeed. Excellent illustrations augment the perceptive analysis.

FRANKLIN THE FOUNDING FATHER

Appleby, Joyce. *Inheriting the Revolution: The First Generation of Americans*. Cambridge, Mass.: Belknap, 2000. Beautifully written, this account explains what a difference the Revolution made.

Bailyn, Bernard. *To Begin the World Anew*. New York: Knopf, 2003. A widely respected historian of early America, Bailyn gives major attention to Jefferson and Franklin, with emphasis on their representation in the arts.

Bowen, Catherine Drinker. *Miracle at Philadelphia*. Boston: Little, Brown, 1966. A highly readable account of the Constitutional Convention.

Ellis, Joseph J. *The Founding Brothers: The Revolutionary Generation*. New York: Knopf, 2001. Ellis gives flesh and blood to the remarkable founders.

Maier, Pauline. *American Scripture*. New York: Knopf, 1997. An excellent treatment of the Declaration of Independence, with its antecedents and imitators.

Morris, Richard B. *The Peacemakers and American Independence*. New York: Harper and Row, 1965. A thorough and careful examination of the work of Franklin and others in bringing an end to the American Revolution

Tourtellot, Arthur B. *Lexington and Concord: The Beginning of the War of the American Revolution*. New York: W. W. Norton, 1963. In captivating detail, this study offers the clearest picture of the initial phase of the American Revolution.

Wood, Gordon S. *The Radicalism of the American Revolution*. New York: Knopf, 1992. Wood makes a solid case for the Revolution as a bold and daring event.

FRANKLIN THE SCIENTIST

Cohen, I. Bernard. *Benjamin Franklin's Science*. Cambridge, Mass.: Harvard University Press, 1990. The most authoritative treatment of Franklin as scientist.

Dray, Philip. *Stealing God's Thunder: Benjamin Franklin's Lightning Rod and the Invention of America*. New York: Random House, 2005. Offers remarkable detail on Franklin as scientist, particularly with respect to electricity.

Goodman, Nathan G. *The Ingenious Dr. Franklin*. Philadelphia: University of Pennsylvania Press, 1931. A useful collection of relevant Franklin letters, with pen-and-ink sketches of some of his inventions.

Index

Page numbers in bold print refer to illustrations and extended extracts from primary sources.

Abolitionism. *See* Slavery

"Account of Negotiations in London" (Franklin), 84

Adams, Abigail, 103, 120

Adams, John, 81, 95, 96, 103, 104, **108–9**, 120

Adams, Samuel, 83

Addison, Joseph, 7

"Address to the Public" (Franklin), 115

African Americans, 77–78. *See also* Slavery

Albany Plan of Action, 57–58, 66

American colonies, 36, 80–81; defense of, 52–54, 92; immigrants to, 17, 55–56, 110–11; proprietors for, 60–63; taxation of, 60–61, 65–67, 71–75, 81; as United States, 95, 99, 105, 110–15; unity of, 57–58, 66, 68. *See also specific colonies*

American Philosophical Society, 33, 41

American Revolution, 89–106; beginnings of, 77; Constitutional Congress, 90–91, 92, 94–98, 103–4, 106; costs of, 92–94, 98–99, 105–6; French society during, 100–102; military activities, 85, 89–90, 98–99

Animal magnetism, 106

Apology for Printers (Franklin), 26

Armonica, **45**

Army, Continental, 92

Articles of Belief & Acts of Religion (Franklin), 117

Articles of Confederation, 112–13

Autobiography (Franklin), quotes from, 6, 16, 18, 19, 23, 24, 28, 31, 54, 55, 117

Bache, Benjamin Franklin (grandson), 97

Bache, Richard (son-in-law), 76, 91, 92, 93

Banks, Joseph, 42

Bartram, John, 41

Beccaria, Giambatista, 46

Bethlehem (Pennsylvania), 56

Bifocals, 47–48

Book of Common Prayer (Franklin), 117

Boston, 5–11, 19, 89, 98

Boston Gazette, 83

Boston Tea Party, 81, 83

Boycotts, 67, 76

Braddock, Edward, 59–60, 61

Bradford, Andrew, 18

Bradford, William, 15

Brillon, Madame, 102

Britain: Board of Trade, 57; Crown, 54–55, 58, 63–64, 71, 72, 90,

Britain (*continued*)
92; Empire, 75, 110; Parliament,
58–59, 63–67, 71–75, 84; peace
talks, 54, 104–5; Privy Council,
80, 82–83; at war, 52, 57, 59,
68–69, 89–90. *See also* American
Revolution
Bunker Hill (Boston, Massachusetts), 98
Bunyan, John, 7
Burgoyne, John "Gentleman
Johnny," 99
Burlington (New Jersey), 16

Canada, 64, 83, 94, 105
Carroll, John, 106
Catholic Church, 106, 122
"Causes of the American Discon-
tents, The" (Franklin), 72, 74
Christianity, 118
Chronology, 127–30
Church of England, 122
Civic improvement, 35–36
Class structure, 111
Clinton, George, 54
Coercive Acts (Intolerable Acts), 83
Colden, Cadwallader, 30
College of Philadelphia, 49
Collinson, Peter, 37, 39–40, 55
Colonies. *See* American colonies
Common Sense (Paine), 93, 94
Concord (Massachusetts), 85, 89–
90
Confederation Congress, 112
Constitution, U.S., 114–15, 124
Constitutional Convention, 112–14
*Constitutions of the Free-Masons,
The* (Franklin), 24–25
Continental Army, 91–92

Continental Congress: first, 83–84;
second, 90–91, 92, 94–97, 103–
4, 106, 108
Cornwallis, Charles, 104
Crown, British, 54–55, 58, 63–64,
71, 72, 90, 92. *See also specific
kings*
Currency, **113**
Cushing, Thomas, 77

Dartmouth, Lord William, 77
Daylight saving time, 46–47
Deane, Silas, 97, 102
Declaration of Independence, 96
Declaratory Act, 75
Delaware Indians, 63
Democracy, symbol of, 100
"Dialogue Between Two Presbyteri-
ans" (Franklin), 25
Diderot, Denis, 102
Discussion club (Junto), 22–23
*Dissertation on Liberty and
Necessity,* (Franklin), 20
Dr. Bray's Associates, 78

Eagle, as national symbol, 106
East India Company, 83
Education and self-improvement, 5–
9, 20–24, 44, 48–49, 55–56, 77–
78, 115–17
Electricity, 36–40, 50–51, 112
England. *See* Britain
Essays to Do Good (Mather), 9
Europeans, in America, 110
*Experiments and Observations on
Electricity Made at Philadelphia
in America* (Franklin), 39

Firefighting, 35
First Continental Congress, 83–84

France, 52, 54, 59, 68, **101**, 108; as ally to America, 97–99, 104; French and Indian War, 57, 64, 71, 98

Franklin, Abiah (mother), 5

Franklin, Anne (first wife of Josiah), 5

Franklin, Benjamin, 136 n.7; abolitionist, 115–16, 124–25; birth and childhood, 5–8; in Boston, 5–11, 19; and charge of treason, 76–77, 80; chronology, 127–30; colonial agent, 66–67, 80–81; commissioner to Canada, 94; in Constitutional Convention, 112–14; death and funeral, 119–22; editor, 10–11; education and self-improvement, 5–9, 20–24, 44, 48–49, 55–56, 77–78, 115–17

Franklin, Benjamin, opinions on: cultures, 117; economy, 46–47; education, 8–9, 44, 48–49, 55–56, 77–78, 115; freedoms, 11; frugality, 100; heroes, 2–3; hooped petticoats, **13–14**; language, 55–56; lighthouses, 42–43; morality and virtues, 23–24, **31–32**; patents, 34–35, 40; philosophy, 33–34; proprietors, 60–61, 63; public opinion, **86–87**; religion, 9–10, 20–21, 25–26, 28, 56–57, 117–18, 122; slavery, 78–79, 115–16

Franklin, Benjamin, scientific pursuits: animal magnetism, 106; bifocals, 47–48; daylight savings time, 46–47; electricity, 36–40, **50–51**, 112; gout treatment, 48; Gulf Stream, 43–44, 85; heat absorption, 44; musical instruments, 44–45; stove, 34–35

Franklin, Deborah Read (wife), 6, 7, 9–11, 16, 19, 20, 24, 65, 76, 88, 119

Franklin, Franky (son), 24, 119

Franklin, James (brother), 6, 7, 9–11, 19

Franklin, Josiah (father), 5–6, 11

Franklin, Sarah "Sally" (daughter), 24, 76, 100

Franklin, Temple (grandson), 84–85, 97

Franklin, William (illegitimate son), 24, 61, 64, 92–93, 106

Franklin stove, 34–35

Freedoms, 11, 73

Freemasons, 24–25, 101

French and Indian War, 57, 64, 71, 98

Frugality, 100

Gage, Thomas, 77, 89, 91

Galloway, Joseph, 82

Gentleman's Magazine, 39

George III (king), 64, 71, 90, 92, 98, 99, 121

George II (king), 60

Gérard, Marguerite, **121**–22

Germans, 55–56

Glass armonica, **45**

Gout treatment, 48

Great Compromise, 113–14

Grenville, George, 66

Gulf Stream, 43–44, 85

Hall, David, 30, 66

Harvard College, 8, 40

Heat absorption, 44

Helvétius, Madame, 102

Hemphill, Samuel, 25

Heroes, 2–3

Honorary degrees, 40–41
Hot-air balloon, 41–42
House of Commons, 63, 73, 75
House of Lords, 75
House of Representatives, 113
Howe, Richard, 75, 96
Howe, William, 98
Hume, David, 63, 102
Hutchinson, Thomas, 76–77, 82

Immigrants to America, 17, 55–56, 110–11
Independence, 63, 75, 79, 92, 94–96, 105. *See also* American Revolution
Indians. *See* Iroquois Indians; Native Americans
Information to Those Who Would Remove to America (Franklin), 110
Intolerable Acts (Coercive Acts), 83
Inventions. *See* Franklin, Benjamin, scientific pursuits; *specific inventions*
Iroquois Indians, 57, 58

Jay, John, 104, 107
Jefferson, Thomas, 49, 92, 95, 104, 106, 120
"Join or Die" (Franklin), 59, **68**
Journal of Paris, 46
Junto (discussion club), 22–23

Kames, H. H., 72
Keimer, Samuel, 18, 19, 21
Keith, William, 18–19, 20
King George's War, 54–55
Kinnersley, Ebenezer, 37
Kite experiments, 38, 40

Lamp globe design, 36
Landlords, absentee (proprietors), 60–63
Langdon, John, 124
"Late Benjamin Franklin, The" (Twain), 1
Laurens, Henry, 104
Lee, Arthur, 97, 102
Le Roy, Julien-David, 44
Letters from an American Farmer, 123
Lexington (Massachusetts), 85, 88–90
Library Company of Philadelphia, 22
Lighthouses, 42–43
Lightning, 38–39, 50–51
Lightning rod, 39, 50
Livingston, Robert R., 108
London, public opinion in, 86–87
London Chronicle, 78, 86
Louis XVI (king), 98

Madison, James, 112, 114, 120
Manufacturing, British and American, 74
Masons, 24–25, 101
Massachusetts, 6, 81, 83, 85, 88–90, 98, 106, 112. *See also* Boston
Mather, Cotton, 9
Meredith, Hugh, 20
Mesmerism, 106
Military activities, 53–55, 84–85, 89–90, 92, 98–99. *See also* American Revolution; French and Indian War; *and specific battle sites*
Mob violence, 66
Morality, 23–24, 31–32
Moravians, 56–57

Morris, Robert H., 60
Musical instruments, 44–45

Native Americans, 59, 71, 116–17;
    Delaware, 63; French and Indian
    War, 57, 64, 71, 98; Iroquois, 57,
    58
New England, 54, 76
New-England Courant, The, 8, **10**–
    11
New Jersey, 64
New York City, 98
New York state, 12, 15, 73, 99
Norris, Isaac, 62

"Of Lightning, and the Method
    (Now Used in America) of
    Securing Building and Persons
    From Its Mischievous Effects"
    (Franklin), 50
Oliver, Andrew, 76–77
"On the Propriety of Taxing
    America" (Franklin), 71
Oxford University, 41

Pacifism and pacifists, 52, 55
Paine, Thomas, 93–94
Paris, Peace of (1763), 64
Paris, Treaty of (1783), 105
Parker, John, 89
Parliament, British, 58–59, 63–67,
    84; and right to tax, 65–67, 71–
    75. *See also* House of Lords;
    House of Commons
Patents, 34–35, 40
Peace talks, 54, 104–6
Penn, Thomas, 60–62, 63
Penn, William, 17, 60, 62, 116
Pennsylvania, 17–18, 49, 52, 56, 60,
    62, 96

Pennsylvania Assembly, 29, 60–61,
    63–64
Pennsylvania Gazette, 21, 25, 29,
    58, 68
Pennsylvania Society for Promoting
    the Abolition of Slavery, 115,
    124
Peters, Richard, 62
Philadelphia, 22, 35–36, 53–54, 65,
    83; Franklin in, 15–20, 25, 29,
    85, 88, 112
Philadelphia Charity School, 78
Philosophy, 33–34
Pilgrim's Progress (Bunyan), 7
Plain Truth (Franklin), 53
"Plan for the Union of the Colonies"
    (Franklin), 57
Poor Richard Improved (Franklin),
    33
Poor Richard's Almanack (Franklin),
    2, 5, 15, **27**–29, 33, 52, 70, 88,
    110
Population, vote and, 113
Postal system, 29, 51, 83, 91
Presbyterianism, 25
Price, Richard, 122
Priestley, Joseph, 63, 91
Printing, 15, 18, 21, 26–30, 103
Privy Council, 80, 82–83
*Proposal for Promoting Useful
    Knowledge Among the British
    Plantations in America*
    (Franklin), 35
*Proposals Relating to the Education
    of Youth in Pennsylvania*
    (Franklin), 48–49
Proprietors, colonial, 60–63
Public opinion, 26, 65–66, 79, 86–
    87

Quakers (Society of Friends), 17–18, 52, 55, 63, 79
Quartering Act, 73
"Queries" (Franklin), 86

Read, Deborah (wife of Franklin), 6, 7, 9–11, 16, 19, 20, 24, 65, 76, 88, 119
Rebellion. *See* American Revolution
Religion, 5, 9–10, 20–21, 25, 28, 56–57, 78, 106, 117–18, 122. *See also* Quakers
"Remarks" (Franklin), 116
Representation, taxation without, 66–67
Republicanism, 94
Retreat, Washington's, 98–99
Revere, Paul, 89
Revolutionary battles. *See* American Revolution; Bunker Hill; Concord; Lexington; Saratoga
Rights: of Declaratory Act, 75; of proprietors, 63; threatened, 73; treaty, 105
Rittenhouse, David, 41
Rogers, John, 24
Roman Catholic Church, 106, 122
Royal Academy of Sciences, 101–2
Royal Society of London, 39, 40–41
Rules by Which a Great Empire May Be Reduced to a Small One (Franklin), 79–80
Rutledge, Edward, 96

St. Andrews University (Scotland), 41
Saratoga, victory in (New York), 99
Satire, 1–2, 7–8, 79–80, 116–17

Saunders, Richard, 27. *See also* Poor Richard's Almanack
Second Continental Congress, 90–91, 92, 94–97, 103–4, 106, 108
Self-improvement and education, 5–9, 20–24, 44, 48–49, 55–56, 77–78, 115–17
Senate, U.S., 113
Shays's Rebellion, 112
Sherman, Roger, 95
Silence Dogood, 8–9, 13
Slavery, 77–78, 115–16, **124–25**
Smith, William, 120
Society of Friends (Quakers), 17–18, 52, 55, 63, 79
Sons of Liberty, 66
Spain, 52, 54, 59, 64, 104
Stamp Act, 65–67, 70, 73–75
Stamp Act Congress, 66
States. *See* American colonies; *specific states*
State sovereignty, 113
Steele, Richard, 7
Stevenson, Margaret, 61
Stevenson, Polly, 44, 61
Stiles, Ezra, 117–18
Street paving, 35–36

Taxation, 60–61, 81; Parliament and, 65–67, 71–75. *See also* Stamp Act; Townshend duties
Thomson, Charles, 82
Thunder, 50–51
Townshend, Charles, 75
Townshend duties, 75, 81
Transatlantic crossings, 20–21, 42, 84–85, 88–89, 97, 106
Treaty of Paris (1783), 105
Turgot, Baron, 100, 102, 122
Twain, Mark, 1–2

United States, 95, 99, 105, 110–15. *See also* American colonies; *specific states*
University of Pennsylvania, 49
University of Virginia, 49

Vasseur, Charles Le, 122
Vatican, 106
Vergennes, Comte de, 97.104, 105
Virginia, 41, 49, 94–95, 104
Virtues, 23–24, 31–32
Voltaire (François-Marie Arouet), 101–2
Volunteer fire companies, 35
Vote, proportional, 113

War, 52, 54–55. *See also* American Revolution; French and Indian War

Waring, John, 78
War of Independence. *See* American Revolution
Washington, George, 59, 91, 92, 98–99, 112–13, 115, 120, 136n.8
Washington, Martha, 120
Wedderburn, Alexander, 81, 82, 83
West, Benjamin, **38**, 40
Whaling, 43
Whately, Thomas, 76–77
Whatley, George, 48
Whitefield, George, 26, 77–78
William and Mary College, 41
Wilson, James, 114

Yale College, 40
Yorktown (Virginia), 104